THEY PLAYED FOR

LAUGHS

Dear Sally & Bob,

Was great seeing you at Homecoming. Hope you like the book.

Jim Brewer

The True Story of Stewart Ferguson and the Arkansas A&M Wandering Weevils, College Football's "Marx Brothers"

JIM BREWER

outskirts press

Outskirts Press, Inc.
http://www.outskirtspress.com

Paperback ISBN: 978-1-9772-3704-0
Hardback ISBN: 978-1-9772-3705-7

TABLE OF CONTENTS

Author's Foreword

College football is serious business.

What began on November 6, 1869, as a diversion for a group of students from Rutgers and Princeton has become a multi-billion dollar industry, replete with the corruption and blurred values that follow big money.

Today, the sport's major powers receive millions of dollars in revenue from television, ticket and memorabilia sales. Head coaches at the largest universities are routinely signed to multi-year, multi-million dollar contracts, presiding over programs that bring national exposure to their schools while creating a sub-culture of boosters and fans who are more than willing to ignore the sport's rules and governing body, the NCAA, to make sure their school wins – and wins big.

In the last 20 years alone, USC's Reggie Bush became the first player in the 85-year history of the Heisman Trophy to return the coveted award for accepting benefits that included a $757,500 house for his parents supplied by a professional sports agency; Cecil Newton, father of 2010 Heisman winner Cam Newton admitted to shopping his son to Mississippi State for $180,000; Ohio State coach Jim Tressel resigned after admitting to covering up NCAA violations by several star players, including quarterback Terrell

Pryor; rogue booster Nevin Shapiro admitted to an eight-year run of NCAA rule-breaking at the University of Miami, providing Hurricane players with cash, prostitutes, jewelry, bounties for on-field play, travel, and on one occasion, an abortion, prompting *Sports Illustrated* to call on former UM President Donna Shalala to shut down the football program. Most recently, the University of Mississippi saw reduced scholarships and a bowl ban for repeated recruiting violations.

But those violations of NCAA rules seem minor in the wake of a shocking child sex abuse scandal at Penn State, a story that rocked college football to its foundation in 2011. Long-time Nittany Lions assistant coach Jerry Sandusky was convicted of multiple counts of sexual assault on underage boys. Penn State's lack of action when provided with damning information about Sandusky's transgressions cost President Graham Spanier and Athletic Director Tim Curley their jobs. Those dismissals paled when the Penn State Board of Trustees fired iconic football coach Joe Paterno, the most successful coach in the history of the sport, a man known as much for his integrity as his record 409 victories. Paterno's puzzling decision to tell only Curley about a reported incident of abuse, then failing to notify law enforcement authorities, left his once spotless legacy in tatters.

Whether Penn State's lack of action reflected a callous "circle the wagons" mentality to protect the program at all costs, or just an appalling lack of communication, a proud university suffered a blow to its reputation that has taken years to overcome.

What happened at Penn State . . . and at Miami, Ohio State, USC and Ole Miss is an indictment of a sport that has become much more than a pleasant diversion for students. College football in the 21st century is big business involving serious money . . . but it wasn't always that way.

Imagine for a moment that you've just settled into your favorite recliner, television remote in hand. Clemson and Alabama are about to decide the national championship at the Superdome in New Orleans.

As Chris Fowler and Kirk Herbstreit prepare to call the action, the Alabama players charge on to the field dressed in their familiar crimson jerseys, white pants and red helmets.

Across the way, Tiger fans wait expectantly for their heroes in orange and purple, but something is amiss. As 80,000 fans look on in disbelief, the Tigers saunter on to the field in their trademark orange helmets, but their jerseys and pants are the same color as the Crimson Tide.

As the game unfolds, bewildered spectators and a national television audience watch Clemson players shuttle from sideline to huddle by bicycle. One of the Tigers leaves the field, climbs into the stands and begins playing the drums with the Alabama band. Late in the first quarter, the Tigers drive to the Alabama two-yard line, only to punt backwards. At halftime, a bored Clemson coach Dabo Swinney leaves the stadium, wanders down Canal Street to the French Quarter and orders a plate of beignets and coffee at the Café du Monde.

As the third quarter begins, Clemson players grab a Bama cheerleader and order him to kick off. When Swinney returns midway through the third quarter, most of his players (at least those not on the field) are in the Alabama student section chatting up the coeds. In the television booth high above the playing field, Fowler and Herbstreit are speechless.

When the game mercifully comes to an end, Alabama has slaughtered the Tigers 61-0.

It's an outlandish fantasy that couldn't happen today, but seven decades ago, when college football was less sophisticated . . . and far less important, it *did* happen.

Not at the Superdome, but at smaller stadiums from Long

Island to California. It happened thanks to a soft-spoken coach and a strange band of football vagabonds known as the "Wandering Weevils."

From 1939 to 1941, the football team from tiny Arkansas A&M College – the Boll Weevils – traveled the country from coast to coast, playing football for fun. Their coach, Stewart Ferguson, was also a professor of history, a man who thumbed his nose at college football's establishment and played the game on his terms.

His players were country boys from the segregated South and most had never been more than 10 miles from home. For three seasons, they traveled thousands of miles in an old battered school bus. Along the way they met movie stars and politicians, stood on the shores of both the Atlantic and Pacific Oceans, and were awestruck by the Grand Canyon and the steel and concrete canyons of New York.

They became national sensations. Sportswriters of the day called them the Marx Brothers of college football. They rode bicycles from sideline to huddle and stood at attention with their helmets removed as enemy ball carriers raced through them for touchdowns. They tackled their own quarterback, quacked like ducks in the rain, and serenaded fans with their own version of "You Are My Sunshine."

They lost most of the time, but Ferguson didn't care and neither did his players. When it was over, when the Wandering Weevils had played their last game on November 26, 1941, the young men who played football for a lark were soon thrust into military service.

Modern college football should take note of Stewart Ferguson and the Wandering Weevils. They truly didn't care whether they won or lost; they played the game strictly for fun, with no illusions of personal glory and certainly not money. Ferguson held to the quaint notion that the sport should be an enriching experience for his players, not a win-at-all-costs battle for survival. As big-time college football struggles with corruption, maybe it's time for the sport to pause and consider the Wandering Weevils and the lessons that can be learned from the sport's most unusual team.

Jim Brewer
November 11, 2020

PROLOGUE: NOVEMBER 16, 1940

Stewart Ferguson shoved his hands deeper into the pockets of his overcoat, bracing against the frigid afternoon wind that swept across Long Island from the Atlantic Ocean less than three miles away.

Standing on the sidelines at Hofstra Stadium in Hempstead, New York, Ferguson watched his boys from tiny Arkansas A&M College play what loosely resembled a football game with the Hofstra Flying Dutchmen. The date was November 16, 1940, and in less than two years, the Boll Weevils – or as they were known in the national press – the Wandering Weevils, had become coast-to-coast sensations. Ferguson believed the game should be played for fun and his team resorted to unorthodox formations, wild plays and on-field pranks that left friends and foes alike convulsed in laughter or scratching their heads in bewilderment.

Collier's magazine labeled them the "Marx Brothers of College Football" and newspaper headline writers struggled for adjectives to describe Ferguson's team – "A Circus Without Fleas," "The Nuttiest Team in Football," and "Fergie's Wacky Eleven."

Ferguson cancelled home games and took his team thousands

of miles in a battered green school bus, playing much larger opponents from New York to California while collecting game guarantees that helped the football program turn a profit.

Now, as Ferguson watched the game unfold, he did so quietly, with little emotion. He was nominally the head coach but did little or no coaching during games, sometimes climbing into the grandstands to munch peanuts or chain-smoke. His players called whatever play they wanted and if the play they wanted wasn't in the playbook, they drew one up in the dirt. It was up to the players to determine who started and who played. It was up to Ferguson to make sure the team got to its destination on time and to collect the paycheck after the Weevils had absorbed another beating.

Today, that beating would be by the respectable score of 30-14 to a Hofstra team in just its fourth year of competition. It was the Weevils' eighth loss in nine games, but the players didn't seem to mind and why should they. As a trade-off for losing football games, they were going places, seeing sights and meeting people they'd only seen or read about in magazines and newspapers. Most of the players were country boys and many had never been outside the borders of Arkansas. Now they were touring Revolutionary and Civil War battlefields, gawking at skyscrapers in New York, hobnobbing with radio and motion picture stars, and seeing natural wonders like the Grand Canyon and the redwood forests of California.

It wasn't much of a trade-off. It was, in fact, a great deal for the players. "You just kind of bought into it," remembered Frank Carson, Jr., more than 70 years later. Carson – "Buddy" to his teammates – was a halfback on the 1940 and '41 teams. "The losing didn't bother us. We were having too good a time."

For his part, Ferguson had come to view coaching and college athletics in general with contempt. He viewed sports as the prostitution of the "fine spirit and high ideals of youth for the winning of a coach's reputation, the athletic fame of a college, or the financial gain of bettors."

Ferguson had once coached and played the game to win. He was respected by his coaching peers after building winning teams as a high school coach in Louisiana and giving his alma mater, Dakota Wesleyan University, the best five-year record of athletic competition in its history.

But Ferguson became disillusioned by the hypocrisy of two-faced administrators and boosters, by slush funds and broken promises to players. When he was fired by Dakota Wesleyan in 1934, he thought he was through coaching. A year later, after being hired to coach football and teach history at Arkansas A&M, he was fired after one winless season and told himself that if he ever coached again, it would be on his terms.

Ferguson stayed at A&M, content in the life of a college professor until 1938, when A&M President Marvin Bankston begged him to save a football program beset by scandal and on the verge of financial collapse. Ferguson agreed, with the stipulation that he didn't have to win a game for three years.

After another winless season in 1938, Ferguson decided to thumb his nose at the college football establishment. He would give the game back to the players and they would play the game strictly for fun. He conceived the outrageous idea of turning football games from serious sport into comedy.

For the next three seasons, Ferguson served as the ringmaster of a traveling football circus that lived by their coach's oft-quoted line: "We'll trade a laugh for a touchdown anytime."

Ferguson was an enigma who evoked strong responses from friend and foe alike, a quirky iconoclast who didn't seem to care what others thought. To some, he was a brilliant innovator; to others a man who was either crazy or hated football, or both. His detractors in Monticello, and he had many, considered him a washed-up has-been hell-bent on destroying the game and the reputation of Arkansas A&M. In truth, Ferguson loved football and wanted to save the sport from the excess of overemphasis. Love him or hate him, he did things his way and stands alone in the annals of coaching as a man who truly didn't care if he won or lost.

So just who was this peculiar coach named Ferguson?

CHAPTER 1

Born To Coach

Sweat dripped from Stewart Ferguson's chin as he peddled his open-centered girl's bicycle 12 miles across the monotonous prairie separating Mt. Vernon and Mitchell, South Dakota. The year was 1916 and the 16-year-old Ferguson was on his way to see his first football game, a contest between Dakota Wesleyan University and Madison Normal College.

As a weary Ferguson wobbled onto the Dakota Wesleyan campus perspiring heavily in the unseasonable late September heat, he spotted a white-striped football field with cheaply constructed bleachers on one side. The field itself was a barren stretch of earth with a few sprigs of buffalo grass.

The game had already begun and the home team was in control. Ferguson was fascinated with football and thrilled by the physical contact. The son of a Methodist minister, he had been raised to turn the other cheek, but the thought of being able to kick the hell out of someone in football seemed much more appealing.

As the game unfolded, Ferguson imagined himself on the field racing for touchdowns and delivering thunderous hits on enemy ball carriers. "I'll be the darndest football player Wesleyan ever had," he thought to himself.

And just like that, on the sidelines of a non-descript football field in the middle of nowhere, Ferguson had found his life's calling. He would be a football player and when his playing days were done, a coach.

But first things first. As he walked around the field during half-time dreaming of future football glory, Ferguson's reverie was interrupted by a friend, also the son of a Methodist minister. The friend suggested they walk under the bleachers to look up the skirts of the Dakota Wesleyan coeds.

For perhaps the last time in his life, Ferguson declined to pursue the sins of the flesh. His mind was on football. Ferguson saw the sport as the closest thing to the life and death struggle of war and more exciting than any activity outside the bedroom.

Stewart Alfred Ferguson was born January 27, 1900, in Carthage, Missouri – the oldest of four boys – to William and Edith Ferguson. The family moved to the South Dakota prairie when Stewart was 11 so that William Ferguson could serve as pastor for churches in Gregory, Murdo, and Mount Vernon.

Ferguson's mother, Edith, wanted her oldest son to follow his father into the ministry but by the time young Stewart reached 16, it was apparent his interests lay elsewhere. He had been suspended permanently from the local high school after a confrontation with the school's superintendent. Ferguson was sleeping in study hall one day when the superintendent decided to wake him up by throwing a piece of chalk at the slumbering student, hitting him in the head. Ferguson's hot Irish temper got the best of him and he responded by pulling an ink bottle from his desk and hurling it at the superintendent, hitting *him* in the head. Ferguson was sentenced to working around the parsonage, doing dishes and cleaning house while his embarrassed parents decided what to do with him. In the meantime, young Stewart was sneaking cigarettes and had already had his first sexual liaison, a frightening experience with the Fergusons' hired girl, a large-breasted Bohemian. As he sat in church each Sunday morning, Ferguson decided the road to hell described by his father sounded like more fun than the alternative.

When Ferguson returned from Mitchell, he informed his parents that Dakota Wesleyan had an academy for high school students. As the family sat down for supper, Ferguson announced that he wanted to attend Dakota Wesleyan Academy to study the ministry.

Ferguson's mother was thrilled, but his father, who was aware of his son's fascination with football, saw through the ruse. "If football is the way to the Lord's work," he said, "your mother and I will help."

The next Monday, Ferguson enrolled at Dakota Wesleyan with the tuition and one month's room-and-board paid by his father. Ferguson held multiple jobs to help pay for school, including working as an errand boy for a woman he later described as a "middle-aged somewhat nymphomaniacal widow." After enrolling he immediately headed to the gymnasium and waited for hours for the first football practice.

The coach, a speech professor named Wilds, was a tall, slender, overly-dramatic sort who loved to deliver emotional pep talks but knew little about football. The team rarely practiced and won no games that fall, but the rail-thin Ferguson, who carried barely 135 pounds on a 5-foot 8-inch frame, established himself as one of the team's more aggressive players.

In 1917, with 18-year-old American boys on the way to France to fight Kaiser Wilhelm, Ferguson and his Academy teammates were promoted to the Dakota Wesleyan college varsity. Ferguson made the starting lineup and played the game in an angry mood. Typically one of the smaller players on the field at any time, Ferguson made up for his lack of stature with cheap shots and generally dirty play. Officials usually let Ferguson get away with these shenanigans, thinking him too small to inflict serious damage.

Ferguson enlisted in the Army in 1918 but was released the same year. Returning to Dakota Wesleyan, Ferguson continued his questionable on-field tricks until players from the University of South Dakota had had enough and sent him to the sidelines unconscious. He woke up in the training room with a throbbing headache and a loud roar in his ears.

As the 1919 season approached, Ferguson was excited by the prospect of being the team's starting quarterback. Although technically still a high school senior, Ferguson had two years starting experience on the college varsity and would call the plays in cooperation with head coach Bud Dougherty, a hot-tempered Irishman. The first opponent was Northern State Teachers College at Aberdeen, South Dakota and Ferguson was concocting a play he had been dreaming about for months. Four years earlier on the same field, Dakota Wesleyan's Mark Payne had boomed a 63-yard drop-kick field goal, a national collegiate record. Ferguson wanted to break Payne's mark, a preposterous thought considering Ferguson struggled to kick the ball over the crossbar from 20 yards.

Dakota Wesleyan won the toss and chose the goal with the wind behind them. When Northern State's first possession ground to a halt, Ferguson retreated to receive the punt, purposely letting the ball roll to the goal line before picking it up. Ferguson was intent on not advancing the ball past his own 30-yard line. He wanted his drop-kick to cover 70 yards because "people remember the even numbers."

As Ferguson reached the 30, he was brushed by a Northern State defender and fell to the ground. With visions of national headlines crowding out his common sense, Ferguson retreated into kicking position and barked a series of signals indicating a kick was coming. His astonished linemen turned and glared, but Ferguson just repeated the signals, this time louder and with more authority. The snap was clean. Ferguson dropped the ball nose down and swung his leg. The ball wobbled weakly to the line of scrimmage.

"You, you, you dumb sonofabitch," screamed Dougherty. "Come off that field."

A quarterback no longer, Ferguson was moved to end. He played four more years of college football (eligibility rules were vague to nonexistent at the time), helping the Tigers to South Dakota Intercollegiate Conference championships in 1919, '21, '22, and '23 and was named to several all-conference teams.

Ferguson's behavior off the field reflected his on-field persona. A cocky, chain-smoking, inveterate skirt chaser, he was suspended several times and threatened with expulsion for a variety of misdeeds. He and a friend dressed as females to sneak into the girls' dormitory. After being dressed down in practice by a coach, Ferguson proceeded to tell the coach exactly what he thought of *him*. Once, while giving a speech in the college chapel, Ferguson forgot part of his oration and cursed out loud. He tricked his absent-minded and almost blind history professor into reading a particularly scandalous passage from *Tom Jones*. Called into the college president's office, Ferguson admitted to 11 rules violations, each with the penalty of expulsion. Somehow, he managed to talk his way back into school, thanks in large measure to the fact that he was a brilliant, if undisciplined student who showed real academic promise. By his senior year, Ferguson had been chosen as Dakota Wesleyan's nominee for a Rhodes Scholarship.

Ferguson would go on to earn a master's degree and Ph.D. from Louisiana State University, but as he prepared for graduation in the spring of 1924, he was more concerned about his immediate future. Career choices were limited for English majors from small denominational colleges. Most chose the ministry or teaching. Ferguson knew he would never be a preacher, but teaching also meant the opportunity to coach. Ferguson sent applications across the country before he was contacted by the parish superintendent of DeRidder, Louisiana with an offer of $150 a month to coach and teach. Ferguson eagerly accepted the offer and headed to the Deep South on the first leg of one of the most unusual odysseys in coaching.

CHAPTER 2

ON THE BAYOU

As Ferguson rode the train south through Sioux City, Omaha and Kansas City, he pictured Louisiana as an exotic paradise and passed the time daydreaming of the championships he would win.

When he stepped off the train in DeRidder, it wasn't quite the paradise he'd expected. A sawmill town deep in the pine forests of southwestern Louisiana, the place smelled of resin and sawdust. Ferguson went straight to the superintendent's office to announce his arrival. "I'm the new coach from South Dakota," Ferguson told the Beauregard Parish superintendent. "Fine, fine," answered D. G. Lunsford, "but what made you think we might put you in a Negro school."

Ferguson had placed one condition on his acceptance of the position – that he be sent to a white school. "I just wanted to be sure that my first job would give me a chance to do some real coaching, and I wouldn't know how to begin with Negroes."

In Ferguson's defense, he had probably never seen, much less met, an African-American in South Dakota and was saddled with the inherent racial prejudices of the day.

"You have a white school in a good community," said Lunsford, "and I'm sure with your help, they'll have another good basketball team this year."

Ferguson didn't know much about basketball but promised to deliver a good football team. "I'm sorry," said Lunsford, "but Dry Creek has never had a football team."

Dry Creek was a wide spot in the road 22 miles from DeRidder. Ferguson had traveled 1,500 miles to coach and teach in a country schoolhouse. He thought briefly of resigning on the spot, but the reality of being broke and a long way from home changed his mind.

Ferguson taught Latin and English at Dry Creek High School and was soon promoted to assistant principal in addition to serving as basketball coach. His team played from September to June on an outdoor court frequented by cows and hogs and never lost a game at home.

Ferguson grew to like Dry Creek, mostly for its simple, uncomplicated people. Years later, he admitted to regret at leaving. "The people were really normal and sensible before, during, and after athletic contests," he remembered. "This gave them a high I.Q. in sports even though some were unable to read or write. They knew little about the technical knowledge of sports, as most people don't, but they were willing to admit that they didn't. It's the fans who think they know and don't who, to coaches, are the asses who bray at the sun and the hyenas who laugh at the moon."

Ferguson's success at Dry Creek landed him an offer the next spring from the Lake Charles school district, 50 miles south and light years away from Dry Creek. He would finally get to coach football, as well as basketball and track, for the handsome sum of $3,000 a year.

Lake Charles was everything Dry Creek wasn't – a beautiful town laced with languid bayous and full of history, wealth, culture, and an abundance of outstanding athletes. Ferguson, unlike some coaches, always had the good sense to know that great athletes made great coaches, not the other way around. "I always snicker when I read about a coach making a famous athlete," he observed later, "for I know that God and the boys' parents really did the job. About all any coach can do is set the stage. It takes sexual intercourse to make a great athlete."

Ferguson was right about one thing – good athletes can do wonders for a coach's reputation. Thanks to players like Don Zimmerman and Bill Banker, future All-Americans at Tulane, and Doby Reeves, who later earned All-America honors at LSU, Ferguson enjoyed three years of success at Lake Charles, transforming himself from a self-professed country hick to a coach in high demand.

Ferguson imbued his football team with the same nasty streak he demonstrated as a player. He taught them a number of dirty, but effective tricks, such as the judicious use of the fist, knee and elbow. When the opposing team kicked off, he sent three players at the defenseless kicker, who rarely lasted past his first kick. Ferguson would, and did, bend the rules to the breaking point to win, a character trait he deeply regretted later in life.

Ferguson loved Lake Charles – the climate, the people, the slow southern rhythm of life . . . and what he considered the unusually good-looking females. His master's thesis at LSU was a history of Lake Charles. Ferguson might have stayed longer, but a brief and unsuccessful marriage and the early success he was enjoying as a coach had convinced him he was destined for bigger and better things. When a job offer for more money came from Bolton High School in Alexandria, Ferguson took it.

Bolton was considered the model high school of the South and Principal Scott Brame was an educator ahead of his time. Ferguson loved Brame, who wasn't as concerned with winning as he was with the welfare of the athletes. "He was naive in our present era of sophisticated athletics," Ferguson remembered later, "to believe that sports programs should be conducted for the good of those who participated rather than those who bet on the outcome of the games."

Ferguson's stay in Alexandria lasted less than a year. The next spring, a Western Union courier walked into the coaching offices at Bolton High and handed Ferguson a telegram. The message was stunning. Five years after graduating from Dakota Wesleyan in a career that included suspensions and threats of expulsion for a wide variety of misconduct, his alma mater was asking him to return as its athletic director. In fact, Ferguson would serve as the entire athletic department, coaching the football, basketball and track teams.

He was thrilled. Five years into his chosen career, Ferguson had gone from coaching in an obscure country schoolhouse to leading the athletic program at a respected private college.

The prodigal son was coming home.

CHAPTER 3

COMING HOME

Ferguson should have been on top of the world as his train rolled into Mitchell, South Dakota. Instead, he was consumed by doubt and worry. He had left Dakota Wesleyan in 1924 as something of an outcast, a trouble-maker who graduated in spite of himself. He was reminded of the scripture passage – "No prophet is accepted in his own country." Now it was late August 1929 and Ferguson was wondering if he was really the hot-shot coach his record indicated, or the beneficiary of the talented athletes of south Louisiana.

As Ferguson walked up Main Street he was recognized by a man who, five years earlier, wouldn't have given him the time of day. "Hey Fergie," the man called out. "Glad to see you back. You must have been a plenty hot coach down south."

Buoyed by the recognition and flattery, Ferguson made his way to the campus to meet with President Earl Roadman. Roadman was short, bald, and like most college administrators, knew little about athletics. Ferguson thought he was better suited to sell insurance.

A smiling Roadman greeted Ferguson with compliments on his past success, then laid out his expectations for his new coach.

Dakota Wesleyan had been god-awful in 1928, losing all nine games by lopsided scores while finishing last in the 10-team South Dakota Intercollegiate Conference. Roadman wanted results and he wanted them fast.

Ferguson asked Roadman if a lack of talent was the reason for the poor record. Roadman gave Ferguson the answer he expected but didn't want. "The materiel was all right," Roadman said, "but what a coach. But we permitted the coach to finish the year." To Ferguson, Roadman's response was classic; it was always the coach's fault.

When Ferguson called the squad together a few days later, his worst fears were realized. He'd had better talent at Lake Charles and Alexandria. The boys were small and about the only thing they had accomplished the previous season was chasing opposing ball carriers across the goal line as they scored.

Ferguson would have to resort to every trick in his coaching repertoire to get results from this rag-tag bunch. That night, he called former Dakota Wesleyan teammate Glenn Hubbard, who had played alongside Ferguson for three years and was now selling cars in Huron. Ferguson needed an assistant and thought the tall, gangly, slow-talking Hubbard could spare three hours in the afternoons to help out at practice. Hubbard loved the game and in Ferguson's mind, was the only man he knew who could help him turn a no-talent bunch into a winning football team. Hubbard accepted the offer and Ferguson promptly drove to Huron where he and Hubbard sat up most of the night trying to think of ways to coax a few wins out of a team bereft of talent.

Ferguson and Hubbard would use every psychological ploy known to coaching – and a few that hadn't been tried – to whip the boys into a frenzy and convince them they could overcome any obstacle, no matter how large.

The first obstacle was the opening game of the 1929 schedule.

South Dakota State College was a much larger school than Dakota Wesleyan and looked at the Tigers as a warm-up game. Dakota Wesleyan would earn a small paycheck while serving as cannon fodder.

Ferguson knew his team had no chance, but rather than have his players' morale shattered by a one-sided loss, he resorted to an unusual tactic. As he addressed his squad before the game, he asked them for help. "We need to fool our conference opponents," said Ferguson. (South Dakota State was not in the same conference.) "If we lose, the other schools in our league will think we don't have much of a team." If South Dakota State was going to beat the hell out of his team, Ferguson reasoned, let's let the boys think it was their idea.

The strategy worked. As Ferguson walked off the field after a 49-0 defeat, one of his players trotted up, winked and said, "Boy, did we ever fool 'em today."

1929 and 1930 were miserable, desperate years for most of America, but not for Stewart Ferguson. After the loss to South Dakota State, his under-sized team of losers started to win. Next on the schedule was a trip to Sioux Falls College and Ferguson knew his boys would once again be no match for their opponent in size, experience or ability. Nevertheless, he had a plan.

His players looked jittery in the locker room as they waited for Ferguson to deliver his final instructions. Ferguson stood in front of his team, raised his hand for quiet, then paused for a moment. In a quiet, almost trembling voice, he said, "Boys, I've decided to turn you loose this afternoon. You know what that means."

"You bet. It means we beat the bastards," screamed a freshman manager from a corner of the room.

"No, no," Ferguson corrected him. "Those boys aren't bastards." Then, in a voice that indicated it would be much better to *be* bastards, he said with as much disdain as possible, "They're

Sioux Falls College players."

With that, the players charged out of the dressing room and whipped the "bastards" from Sioux Falls convincingly. It was Dakota Wesleyan's first victory in two years. Now brimming with confidence, the Tigers won three of their next four to set up a November showdown with Northern State Teachers College in Mitchell. Ferguson was sure his team was overmatched, and the night before the game, went to bed with a headache and the knowledge that his team's winning ways would probably come to an end the next day.

Before he could fall asleep, the telephone rang. Could Ferguson come to the Green Lantern Café as quickly as possible?

Waiting at the café were the owner, three waitresses and Ferguson's brother. An hour earlier, the Northern State coach and the referee for the game had been seated together in a booth at the back of the café. Their conversation had been overheard by a waitress who was dozing in the next booth. The waitress began taking notes on a napkin. The first thing she heard was "Hoerauff – bad neck." Louis Hoerauff was one of Ferguson's best players, a halfback who had suffered an injured neck in a scrimmage two days earlier. Ferguson had been sure no one outside his squad knew about the injury. When Dakota Wesleyan had the ball, Northern State could count on a quick whistle to stop play. When Northern State had the ball, the whistle would come much slower. Other Dakota Wesleyan personnel were discussed, particularly those with injuries. Ferguson himself was referred to as a "conceited ass who needs a good beating."

Ferguson asked the waitress to swear to her story in an affidavit and the next morning coach and waitress appeared in the office of a local attorney. Ferguson carried the affidavit with him to the game and just before kickoff, called the referee and Northern State coach to the center of the field, and handed them the waitress's testimony.

Neither said a word as they read the affidavit. "Now, you heels, what have you got to say?" Ferguson asked.

Silence.

"I'm just itching to give this stuff to Paul Swenson, sports editor of the (Mitchell) *Republican*," Ferguson said, "but if I were to feel very happy when the game is over, I might change my mind."

Ferguson wheeled and walked back to his sideline. The game's outcome was now a foregone conclusion. Dakota Wesleyan recorded a surprisingly easy 20-0 win over a listless, out-of-synch Northern State team that couldn't catch a break from the officials.

Ferguson's boys whipped Western Union College in a blinding snowstorm, then tied Yankton College in the season finale to win the conference championship with a 5-2-1 record, a 4-0-1 mark in conference play. Ferguson's team had made the amazing leap from last place to first in one year and the coach was embraced by fans and the community. He was even invited to join the Mitchell Kiwanis Club, a sure sign of local acceptance.

President Roadman was able to throw ice water on Ferguson's celebratory mood a few days later. "It would be too bad," Roadman said, "if we were to have a poor basketball team."

He needn't have worried. Ferguson continued his winning ways, leading the basketball team, which had finished ninth the previous year, to a conference title despite knowing little about the intricacies of the sport. He kicked off the team's best player for insubordination, developed a simple offense based on quick passing, and packed his defense close to the basket. The strategy worked and Ferguson was hailed as a coaching genius by the fans who filled the Corn Palace for games.

When spring arrived, Ferguson led the track team to a third-place finish, giving Dakota Wesleyan the best one-year athletic record of any school in the history of the South Dakota Intercollegiate Conference.

Ferguson's first-year success had some unintended consequences. Flushed with the thrill of winning, the locals established an athletic slush fund to attract good athletes with promises of jobs and tuition money.

Ferguson's recruiting – and the availability of cold cash – persuaded some of the region's best football talent to come to Mitchell. Ferguson surveyed the new talent and surmised that another championship was a lock and decided to reward his team with a trip south. Dakota Wesleyan would open the 1930 season in Baton Rouge, Louisiana against another group of Tigers. Ferguson's team would earn every penny of the $1,500 check LSU was willing to pay for this latter-day version of human sacrifice. Ferguson didn't care. He wanted his boys to learn there was more to the United States than the prairies of South Dakota.

The 76-0 massacre at LSU was soon forgotten as Dakota Wesleyan reached the season's final game, a Thanksgiving Day showdown with unbeaten Yankton College, with a 6-2 record and one conference loss. A win over Yankton would give Ferguson his second straight conference championship.

Dakota Wesleyan was tabbed the heavy favorite by sportwriters, but Ferguson was concerned that some of his players were too busy chasing the blondes and brunettes of Mitchell who were suddenly available to a winning football team to concentrate on the task at hand. Ferguson took his players to a movie the night before the game, then implored them to go to bed (their own) and stay there.

Fearing the worst, Ferguson then climbed in his car and began cruising the streets hoping to catch any of his love-starved players before they expended too much energy. He was particularly concerned with a young blonde divorcee and drove by her apartment several times before stopping and knocking loudly on her front door.

When the door finally opened, a scantily-clad woman whispered, "Oh, oh. It's coach." Then a few seconds later and much louder, "Come on in, coach." Ferguson knew instinctively that her guest had made a hurried exit down the back stairway. "I can't come in," said Ferguson. "I was just checking to see how many touchdowns I'd lost in tomorrow's game."

Ferguson drove back to campus, hoping to catch the guilty party. As he crossed the Milwaukee Central Railroad tracks, he spotted not one, but three of his players beating a hasty retreat. He suspended them all for the next day's game, which Dakota Wesleyan lost 13-0. Ferguson had fallen one game short of a second championship. The irony of Ferguson suspending players for sexual hanky-panky wasn't lost on those who knew him well.

Ferguson's winning ways continued into the winter when his basketball team won the second of what would become four straight SDIC titles while earning a berth in the A.A.U. National Tournament. As the 1931 track season came to a close with a second-place conference finish, Ferguson was ready for the big-time, or so he thought. He sent applications to larger colleges and universities across the country and was both surprised and disappointed when he found no takers. He would be back at Dakota Wesleyan for a third year, but not without a substantial pay raise.

Ferguson went to see President Roadman. "I'm sure other colleges will pay me more than I'm receiving here," Ferguson told Roadman with more than a hint of self-satisfaction.

"They will?" asked a smiling Roadman. "I am always glad when our faculty members can better themselves financially."

Sensing a tactical error, Ferguson began to backtrack. "But I guess you understand that I like Wesleyan and would never leave for just more money."

"Do you mean that you really love Wesleyan?" Roadman asked.

"I sure do," said Ferguson.

"Splendid! Splendid! I'm so glad, because we are suggesting that our most loyal faculty members contribute $100 each to our new financial campaign, and I know those that love Wesleyan will not fail her," Roadman said.

Ferguson's shrewd bargaining for a raise had cost him $100, a harbinger of things to come.

Ferguson's third season at Dakota Wesleyan was less successful than the first two. The football record dipped precipitously to 2-6-1 in '31 but Ferguson thought the success of his basketball team would keep the wolves at bay. The Dakota Wesleyan basketball program was starting to draw national attention and Ferguson hoped to capitalize by scheduling games against some of the nation's top basketball powers. In a letter to Notre Dame, Ferguson offered the Fighting Irish anything they wanted for a game in Mitchell and added that Dakota Wesleyan would gladly play in South Bend for nothing more than a game. Irish Coach George Keogan wasn't about to expose his team to the danger of being upset by a tiny college from South Dakota and answered Ferguson's letter with a single sheet of paper with the word "NO" in all caps at the center of the page.

Ferguson then appealed to a fellow Methodist college, Northwestern University of the Big 10, but Northwestern Athletic Director Tug Wilson told Ferguson the Wildcats would not play for any guarantee and added that "after receiving reports of your play, only Notre Dame or Southern California might be able to defeat you." Ferguson finally persuaded Kansas State to play his team and the Tigers defeated them easily en route to a spectacular 17-0 regular season and a third straight conference championship.

But with Stewart Ferguson, nothing was ever as smooth as it seemed. As his undefeated team prepared for a game at Huron College the next day, Ferguson had just finished packing the equipment when his office phone rang.

"Say, if you're Coach Ferguson, you'd better get the hell out here fast if you want to see one of your players alive," said the angry caller.

"What's the matter?" asked Ferguson.

"I'm telling you, I'm gettin' ready to blow the bastard's brains out, and I want you to know the reason before I do it."

Believing the caller meant business, Ferguson got the man's address, jumped in his car and raced to a house on the west side of the city. When he opened the front door, he was confronted by a large, bull-necked, red-faced man in overalls holding a rifle pointed in the general direction of the offending player.

"My God, what's the matter," Ferguson stammered.

"Plenty's the matter," snorted the gun-toting man. "I just caught this son of a bitch diddling my wife."

Ferguson stared at the man for several seconds, trying to think of a way to placate the angry husband and calm his own nerves. The man's blonde, pale wife sat in a chair across the room, scarcely breathing while the player sat stiffly, lips trembling.

Ferguson finally recognized the man as a frequent visitor to the Corn Palace to watch his team. "Say, brother," said Ferguson, "how about letting me use him in the game tomorrow night? I can't win without him and you know how you like to see us win. I promise to bring him back."

"Bring him back?" growled the man. "All you have to do is carry him away."

Several seconds passed. "Give me a cigarette," the man ordered. Ferguson fumbled in his pocket and realized he had left his cigarettes in his office. The player reached in his back pocket and tossed his pack to the gunman.

Ferguson thought the man didn't really want to kill his player or he would have already pulled the trigger. He might still do it to save face, but Ferguson had an idea. "How would you like this kid to buy you all the cigarettes you smoke the rest of your life?" asked Ferguson.

"Whaddayu mean?"

"I just mean that if you will forget this quite human slip that the kid will keep you in smokes as long as you live."

"How do I know he'll keep his word?"

"I'll guarantee his words with my own," said Ferguson. The man lowered his rifle and Ferguson hustled his player out the door and into his car. Neither Ferguson nor the player spoke as they drove back to campus. The angry husband eventually took a job in another town, relieving both Ferguson and his player of their cigarette obligations.

The Tigers would go on to finish 19-1 after reaching the quarterfinals of the A.A.U. National Tournament. For a coach who professed to know little about the sport, Ferguson had fashioned a sparkling basketball record, but it was football that interested the Methodist ministers who made up most of the Board of Trustees and Athletic Council.

Whether Ferguson was getting bored or was just disappointed at being stuck in Mitchell, something was different as the 1932 football season approached. He did little recruiting that summer, expecting his previous success to attract the state's top players. He was wrong. His team finished a pedestrian 3-5-0 and he might have been fired then but for a fourth consecutive basketball championship.

Despite a 54-12 record in basketball, Ferguson was under withering criticism for the performance of the football team. The Kiwanians and ministers who had slapped him on the back during his first three seasons were nowhere to be found. Ferguson was becoming disillusioned with his job and with coaching and college athletics in general. The cockiness was gone, replaced by indecision and doubt.

As the 1933 football season approached, Ferguson found himself wishing for luck rather than believing, as he had in the past, that he would win by out-coaching his opponents. His players noticed the difference in practice. Ferguson wasn't pressuring his boys with psychological tricks. Gone were lessons in dirty tactics and how to get away with them. There would be no more sessions on how to eliminate the opposing team's best players. He even taught his players how to avoid injuries rather than inflict them.

Ferguson even went so far as to tell Roadman of his change in coaching philosophy. He would no longer make promises to athletes that wouldn't be kept. For several years, Ferguson and the Dakota Wesleyan administration had promised prospective athletes anything they asked for in return for playing for the Tigers. Rarely were the promises kept and Ferguson was tired of lying to his players.

Roadman was not pleased with his coach's sudden attack of conscience.

The 1933 season was a disaster. The Tigers won just once although most of the games were close. Ferguson was convinced that had he resorted to his old ways and sacrificed his new-found ethics, his team might have won most of them. He didn't care. In fact, he was satisfied to go to bed at night knowing he had not sacrificed the health and welfare of his players – or of his opponents – to win a football game.

Noble ideals in another profession, but a recipe for disaster in coaching.

When the season was over, Ferguson sensed his days in Mitchell were numbered. Another winning basketball team did little to quiet his critics. When track season arrived, Ferguson discovered that most of his team had been declared academically ineligible by the Dakota Wesleyan Athletic Committee, a ploy often used at the time to discredit an unpopular coach.

Ferguson had had enough. He went to the Mitchell *Republican* and told the sports editor he was resigning. Roadman, who was on the west coast on a fund-raising trip, wired Ferguson and told him he would not permit him to resign, but that he would fire him if the newspaper story wasn't retracted. Ferguson responded with a wire of his own, telling Roadman to go to hell.

Stewart Ferguson, the hot-shot young coach who had given Dakota Wesleyan the best five years of athletic competition in its history, was leaving South Dakota in disgrace. Before leaving, he managed to mend fences with Roadman enough to persuade his former boss to write a glowing letter of recommendation. He would need it.

CHAPTER 4

BACK TO THE SOUTH

As the rural landscape of Illinois rolled past his train window, Ferguson was lost in thought. A few weeks earlier, he had boarded an eastbound train from Mitchell, South Dakota to Chicago with a daffy scheme to make millions betting on horse races.

He had devised a system that looked foolproof on paper. He would turn pari-mutuel tickets into a fortune and leave coaching forever. No more two-faced boosters and administrators, no more sacrificing his own ethics to win games. Just easy money and all the accoutrements that went with it.

Within weeks, he was broke, reduced to carrying what remained of the money he left South Dakota with in the watch pocket of his trousers.

Faced with the prospect of choosing between his principles and eating, Ferguson answered an ad from a small Arkansas college in search of a coach. The school would pay travel expenses so Ferguson swallowed his pride and hopped on a southbound train.

Now, as the train sped toward Memphis, Ferguson reflected on the life he'd left behind. He kicked himself for squandering a fortune on horses. He thought about an attractive blonde and the moonlight picnics they had shared on the banks of the James River outside Mitchell.

Had it only been a few short years since Ferguson had envisioned himself as the second coming of Knute Rockne? He had been willing to bend, and sometimes break any rule, to sacrifice his players' health if it gave his team an edge. He had been an ego-driven, referee-baiting coach obsessed by winning and the glory that went with gridiron success.

Now, at age 34, he was beaten, disillusioned by the hypocrisy of college athletics. If he was to coach again, it would be on his terms.

Ferguson changed trains in Memphis and continued his journey south through the bleak landscape of the Mississippi delta, arriving in McGehee, Arkansas shortly after dawn. He boarded a bus for the remainder of his journey to Monticello 25 miles to the west on a gravel road strewn with potholes.

When Ferguson arrived at the downtown square in Monticello, he discovered there was no taxi service to the campus, which was just over three miles to the south. Monticello was a sleepy community of less than 4,000 people, the county seat of Drew County in southeast Arkansas. The eastern third of the county was low country, swampy and laced with bayous that stretched into the flat Mississippi delta. The western two-thirds was covered with pine and oak forests, slightly higher in elevation. The region was desperately poor, hit hard by the Depression.

Ferguson roused a young man lounging on the square and persuaded him to take him to the campus. Ferguson had three dollars in his pocket and the erstwhile taxi driver took two of them.

Arkansas A&M College was 25 years old in 1934. The college had been created in 1909 as the Fourth District Agricultural School for the purpose of teaching agriculture, horticulture, and the art of textile manufacturing to students in grades six through 12. In 1923, the school attained junior college status and became the Fourth District Agricultural and Mechanical College after reaching an agreement with the University of Arkansas to begin offering two years of college work. By 1934 the school was known as Arkansas A&M and was offering four-year college degrees on a limited basis. In spite of its remote rural location, A&M had already produced a Rhodes Scholar (James Gaston Williamson, class of '32).

A&M enrolled 500 students that fall and the cost was minimal. Room and board for an entire year was $185 for freshmen and sophomores, $195 for juniors and seniors.

The school had enjoyed only sporadic athletic success. The first football team was organized in 1911 and in their first 23 seasons, the Boll Weevils had posted winning records nine times against an assortment of high school, junior college and college teams. The Boll Weevils played their last game against high school competition on October 9, 1925, a 33-0 loss to Dermott High School. In 1931, the school hired Foy Hammons, the man Ferguson was hoping to replace. Hammons had been the school's most successful coach, winning 13 games in three years, topped by a 7-2-1 record in his first season in 1931, at the time, the best in school history.

Arkansas A&M belonged to the Arkansas Intercollegiate Athletic Association, a loose confederation of small public and private four- and two-year Arkansas colleges. The Boll Weevils rarely traveled outside the state for athletic competition.

The boll weevil became the school mascot in 1925, selected by a vote of the student body. At the time, cotton was still king in Arkansas and in those pre-pesticide days, the boll weevil was the most feared pest in the South.

As Ferguson approached the campus, he was impressed with its wild beauty. The land for the school was once part of a 2,000-acre cotton plantation donated to the state by the family of Judge

William Turner Wells, a Confederate war veteran and early settler in Drew County. In 1875, Wells built a lake on the plantation using out-of-work Irish laborers, then stocked the lake with game fish. The lake became the focal point of the Arkansas A&M campus, whose main buildings were clustered on a low hill, nestled in a grove of pine, oak and magnolia trees. The recently-completed Fine Arts Building, with its 76-foot tower of sandstone and marble, loomed over grounds covered in wild flowers. Ferguson thought it one of the most attractive campuses he had ever seen.

What Ferguson didn't know was that Arkansas A&M, like other small, rural colleges, was struggling to survive the Depression. The athletic program, in particular, was on shaky ground.

Ferguson located the administration building and was told President Frank Horsfall was out of the office. No one knew when he would return.

Ferguson killed time by wandering over to the football practice field. As he sat in makeshift grandstands sweating in the June heat, he surveyed a field overgrown with shoulder-high weeds.

A young man doing maintenance work on the field approached.

"Hello," said Ferguson. "You a student here?"

"Yeah, if you can call this goddamned place a school," said the boy.

"What's wrong with the place?" Ferguson asked.

"Everything."

"How's the football team going to be this year," asked Ferguson.

"You guess," the boy answered. "I suppose they'll try to have a football team, but ain't no one going to play on it."

"Why?" said Ferguson.

"Because they can't fire coach Hammons and get by with it," the boy explained.

"Why'd they fire him," Ferguson asked, now more than a little intrigued.

"Jes to give some sonofabitch from up north a job," the boy said.

"What's wrong about any coach from up north," said Ferguson.

"What's right about any goddamned Yankee?" the boy responded angrily.

Ferguson left it at that and contemplated leaving without meeting the president until he reached in his pocket and felt the lone dollar bill. Faced with the stark reality of his financial situation, he headed back to the administration building, arriving just as a red coupe slid to a stop in the parking lot.

Out of the car stepped Frank Horsfall, tall and gaunt, with flashing blue eyes and no patience for fools. Horsfall had run Arkansas A&M with an iron hand for 24 years, first as principal, then as president. Known as "Chief" by friends and enemies alike, Horsfall was a lightning rod for criticism. He had survived one attempt to have him removed from the presidency in 1925 and by 1934 was embroiled in another controversy that would cost him his job six months later.

Horsfall wasted no time, shoving a contract at Ferguson as soon as they entered Horsfall's office.

"Sign it," Horsfall said.

"Well, I don't know," said Ferguson.

"Don't know *what?*" Horsfall said with a growl. "You got what you came for, didn't you? Sign this contract and don't waste any more of my time."

Ferguson signed. He was now the head football coach at Arkansas A&M College and a member of the history faculty. In fact, Ferguson was the entire athletic department. In addition to his duties as head football coach, he would be the athletics director and head basketball coach.

As Ferguson went to bed that night in an unfinished room in a new men's dormitory, he wondered if he'd traded one coaching grave for another. He faced the prospect of no athletes, college registration two days away, resentment over the dismissal of a popular coach and his status as a Yankee. He gave himself three months before his inevitable firing.

The community's reaction to Ferguson's hiring was what he expected, ranging from disdain to outright anger. He was a Yankee. He'd been fired from his last coaching position. And he was a Yankee.

Another strike against Ferguson; he was not Foy Hammons. Hammons had fashioned a respectable 33-22-8 record in three seasons at Arkansas State and five at Ouachita Baptist College before coming to Monticello in 1931. Hammons had two winning seasons in his three years at A&M and was popular with his players and the student body at large. Hammons had been among a handful of faculty who sided with the students in their battle to get Horsfall to loosen his tight rein on every facet of their lives. Horsfall had persuaded the Board of Trustees to adopt a strict set of rules governing student behavior. No dances were allowed on campus and students were forbidden from attending dances off campus during the school year. Horsfall drew an imaginary line through the middle of campus. Girls stayed on one side of the line, boys on the other, except to attend class or the cafeteria.

"You didn't cross (Horsfall)," remembered Minnie Belle McCain, a 1933 A&M graduate. "You didn't talk to boys. If you passed one, you might say something under your breath, but that was it. And you didn't talk out the window of your dormitory to a boy."

When the students launched a formal protest, Hammons sided with the students. Horsfall refused to renew his contract.

Into the breech stepped Ferguson.

In the fall of 1934, America was still firmly in the grip of the Great Depression. Newspaper headlines that fall were dominated by news of the capture of Bruno Richard Hauptman, who kidnapped and murdered the 20-month-old baby of Charles and Anne Lindbergh in what was labeled "The Crime of the Century." Infamous gangsters Pretty Boy Floyd and Baby Face Nelson were both gunned down by federal agents and the World Series had a distinctly Arkansas flavor with Dizzy and Paul Dean pitching for the St. Louis Cardinals against Schoolboy Rowe of the Detroit Tigers.

Closer to home, Foy Hammons was winning games at Hope High School and Arkansas A&M was preparing to dedicate a new concrete football stadium, a Works Progress Administration project made possible by President Franklin Roosevelt's New Deal.

The first football practice of the 1934 season was scheduled for one week after students registered for fall classes. Eight players reported the first day and to Ferguson's dismay, he could outrun all of them in a 50-yard sprint. Most of the veterans who had played for Hammons initially stayed away. Only five returning lettermen reported the first week, including two all-state performers from the previous season; end Howard Hagaman of Stuttgart, a three-year letterman, and halfback-quarterback Clarence "Sonny" Gordon of Holly Grove, slightly built at 133 pounds but the team's fastest player the previous season. Joining Hagaman and Gordon were tackle Dwight Hobbs of Monticello, end Allan Keith of Stuttgart and end Coy Scifres of Garnett. Frank McGibbony, who had starred on Pine Bluff High School's mythical national championship team in 1925 and played for A&M the previous season, would serve as Ferguson's assistant coach.

When all-conference lineman Van Tuberville returned, it made headlines in the *Pine Bluff Commercial*. *"Tuberville's addition to the squad brings a slightly better feeling to the Bollweevil (sic) fans,"* the paper reported. By the end of the first week of practice, the squad numbered 25 warm bodies, although Ferguson thought only five had the talent of a good high school player.

Ferguson tried to drill his boys in traditional football but knew his squad faced serious limitations. His best defensive player, a 200-pound middle guard, needed a nip of whiskey before every game to encourage his best effort. His fullback weighed 130 pounds and Gordon, though a fast, slashing outside runner, was fragile and injury-prone.

The first game was on the road at Hendrix College, a small Methodist school in Conway, Arkansas, about 30 miles north of the state capital in Little Rock. To Ferguson's surprise, his team played well through much of a scoreless first half, thanks mostly to Gordon's running, passing and punting and a defense that held the Warriors to one first down. A lack of depth finally caught up with his undermanned squad in the second half as Hendrix scored twice in the third quarter and once more in the fourth to win 18-7.

The narrow loss buoyed Ferguson's spirits. Maybe, just maybe, this collection of misfits could be molded into a competitive football team.

His good humor lasted until Sunday morning when he was called before the A&M athletic committee. Many on the committee did not like Ferguson, and had opposed his hiring to replace the popular Hammons. Ferguson had no idea what the meeting was about.

"Did you, Coach Ferguson, pick up Spot Holmes with the college bus on your return from Conway," came the first question from the committee chairman.

"Yes," replied a surprised Ferguson. "What's wrong with that?"

Ferguson had been informed before the trip to Conway not to give rides to hitchhikers on the college bus. During the Depression, hitchhiking was a popular and sometimes necessary means of travel. But Spot Holmes was no hitchhiker, Ferguson said. He was an Arkansas A&M student.

"A hitchhiker is anyone on the highway seeking a means of conveyance," said the agitated chairman.

"You picked up Spot Holmes, and he's a hitchhiker," shouted an irritated language professor.

More outrage ensued. "Will you ever again pick up a hitchhiker?" asked the chairman.

"I guess I will if it's someone like Spot," said Ferguson, now in a defiant mood.

"You've just made a most serious statement," said the chairman. "You are actually defying us. You are excused, Coach Ferguson."

Ferguson couldn't resist a parting shot. "Thanks for this favor," he said and turned for the door.

He was through he was certain, and after just one game. Anger, hurt and disillusionment welled up in Ferguson's throat. He packed his belongings, put them on the school bus and headed to Horsfall's office to tell the president that he and his college could go to hell.

"So, you're going to keep on picking up hitchhikers, eh?" said Horsfall as Ferguson walked through the door. Very little happened on the Arkansas A&M campus without Horsfall's knowledge. Before Ferguson could respond, Horsfall said, quietly, "Ferguson, if you had told that bunch of sorry asses that you wouldn't pick up any more hitchhikers like Spot, I'd have fired you on the spot."

Ferguson was still intent on quitting and said so.

"Like hell you are," Horsfall said with a snarl. "You want to be a damn sissy? Don't you know that men have to knock each other around a bit before they become really acquainted? We're just beginning to know you and you're NOT quitting!"

Frank Horsfall would last only four more months as president at A&M, but he had taught Ferguson a valuable lesson. He would have to fight for his principles . . . and his job.

The next two teams on A&M's schedule were two of the best in the state. Henderson State Teachers College in Arkadelphia and the

College of the Ozarks in Clarksville had the funds to attract plenty of football talent. Both teams scored touchdowns in bunches and A&M's only hope was to play keep-away with an offense based on ball possession.

Ferguson began tinkering with formations until he hit upon an idea. He would place a back close to the line with all the linemen on one side of the ball. The center would line up to the extreme right or left of the remainder of his line, then snap the ball at an angle to the back. The back could begin gaining ground by his second step. As the line pivoted forward (hopefully) the play resembled a swinging gate. Whether Ferguson actually invented the swinging gate or simply adapted something he'd seen elsewhere, the play became a staple of his offense.

The swinging gate did allow for short gains and an edge in first downs, but while the Boll Weevils were making first downs, their opponents were scoring touchdowns. The dedication of the new stadium on October 12 was a disaster. Henderson State, on its way to a third straight conference championship, obliterated A&M 63-0. The next week, Ozarks thumped the Weevils 45-0. The back-to-back home losses brought an increasingly disgruntled fan base. To make matters worse, Gordon suffered a severely sprained ankle against Ozarks in a game marred by rough play.

The losses mounted. A 38-0 shellacking by Arkansas College included an incident that perfectly summed up the Boll Weevils' season. Back-up lineman Oscar "Cab" Calloway was minding his own business on the A&M bench when he was steamrolled and seriously injured by players from both teams.

Next came losses to Arkansas State 19-0, Arkansas Tech 53-0, and Ouachita Baptist 57-0. Ferguson was under intense criticism from the town, the faculty, even his own players. Ferguson's practices weren't long enough; he wasn't tough enough; he didn't cuss and whip his players like coaches were supposed to do.

The season ended in El Dorado in a sea of mud with a 7-6 loss to archrival Magnolia A&M. Ferguson used the game as an object lesson for a pair of particularly rebellious players, holding them out of the game until the final seconds, knowing they might have made the difference between victory and defeat. He was ashamed of himself for sacrificing a potential win to gain a measure of personal revenge.

The 0-8 season was an unmitigated disaster from start to finish. Ferguson's team was outscored 300-13 and managed just two touchdowns, one in the season opener and one in the finale. In between were six lopsided shutouts.

Headlines in the *Arkansas Gazette* during the season rubbed salt in the wound. "Monticello Easy For Ouachita Team" the paper declared after a 57-0 blowout. "Monticello Boll Weevils Try Hard but Look Bad by Comparison" was the headline after a 53-0 loss to Arkansas Tech. William Wilson, the *Gazette's* state editor who wrote the game story, was brutal in his criticism.

"If the Dads of Arkansas Polytechnic College expected to see a real football game on their day of days here today, undoubtedly they were disappointed. Instead they saw their sons literally massacre Monticello A. and M. The score was 53 to 0. And the Techmen easily could have run up a bigger score but Coaches Tucker and Cowan apparently wanted to give the Dads a break. So they sent in the second string men after piling up three easy touchdowns in the first quarter.

"We don't want to leave the impression that the youngsters from Drew County didn't play football — they did, and played well, but so far inferior was the brand to that put up by Tech that it was pitiful. They just didn't have the power and the smartness and the experience it requires to cope with a team such as

that exhibited by Tech . . . Monticello never came near scoring, although the Boll Weevils were within the 20-yard line twice. It really was through accident they got there. But you could tell from the faces of Techmen that there was no real danger of the Russellville line being crossed."

The season left Ferguson on thin ice but attention was momentarily deflected from the football coach to the administration building as the controversy surrounding Horsfall finally reached a breaking point.

In January, Horsfall was out after 25 years. On March 25, the A&M board of trustees announced Horsfall's replacement, former Arkansas Tech and Mississippi State President Hugh Critz. Critz was known for two things, a deep, booming voice and a love of sports. His son, Hughie, had just completed his 11th season in the major leagues as a second baseman, seven with the Cincinnati Reds and now four with the New York Giants. The elder Critz had led both Tech and Mississippi State to football prominence and the locals were hoping for similar results at A&M.

Critz used his first day on the job to call each faculty member to his office and assure them that he wanted them to remain in their jobs, Ferguson included. The locals would have none of that. They wanted Ferguson fired immediately, in spite of his 15-5 record in basketball. To the locals, football was the only sport that mattered.

Critz was too much the politician to cross so many supporters this soon. A few days later, he called Ferguson to his office. "Ferguson, boy, I'm mighty glad to see you," Critz boomed. "Ferguson, I understand you're a crack history teacher."

"I just try to do my best," Ferguson said.

"Now that's something I have always tremendously admired . . . a good history teacher," said Critz. "God knows we need more of them."

Ferguson knew what was coming next.

Critz sprang to his feet. "I'm not going to ruin a good history teacher by making a goddamned football coach out of him," Critz said, practically shouting. "You know as well as I do that they're just a damn bunch of morons. You've got brains."

"But I just want to be a smart football coach," Ferguson mumbled.

"You mean, you mean that I've found someone who'd rather coach football than teach history?" Critz asked.

Yes, Ferguson would rather coach football. He was putting Critz in the position of breaking a promise made days earlier just to placate fans. The two men glared at each other before Critz ended the meeting with a dismissive wave of his hand.

Days later, at a town meeting at the county courthouse, Critz stood up to chart his planned course for the college and the football team. Using the cadence of a polished southern politician, Critz asked his audience if they wanted a good football team.

The response was loud and positive.

"Do you want the present football coach?" Critz asked. Ferguson was at the back of the room and could barely resist the urge to join the screams of "No" coming from the crowd.

That was it. Ferguson was out as football coach, the victim of a public lynching minus the rope. He could remain on the faculty, and since jobs were scarce, he decided to stay. In the next few weeks, he was snubbed by townspeople and faculty he had counted as friends.

He was convinced he had coached his last football game.

CHAPTER 5

BO SHERMAN

Eugene H. "Bo" Sherman was the answer.

Sherman had been a two-way all-state player at Henderson State Teachers College in Arkadelphia, Arkansas in the 1920's before building a football juggernaut at his alma mater in the early 30's, winning three consecutive AIC championships from 1932 to 1934. He was everything Ferguson wasn't – aggressive, a little rough around the edges and willing to break rules when necessary. He was just the man Hugh Critz and the fans of Monticello wanted to lead Arkansas A&M to football glory, never mind that Henderson State had forced Sherman to resign at the end of the '34 season for using ineligible players. Critz, and it seemed everyone else in Monticello, was willing to forgive this minor indiscretion.

"Bo ain't too particular about how he goes about winning games," said one fan, "but he damn sure wins 'em."

Critz couldn't hire Sherman immediately. The previous December, the Arkansas Intercollegiate Athletic Association had suspended Henderson State for "violations of rules and regulations of the conference" and approved a measure prohibiting any conference team from playing a team coached or directed by Sherman.

37

Critz went to work behind the scenes lobbying to have the restrictions on Sherman lifted. In the meantime, Sherman was already on campus "helping" Ferguson coach the football team through spring practice.

By April 27 the conference restrictions on Sherman had been lifted and on May 21, he was formally introduced as Arkansas A&M's director of athletics and head football coach. Ferguson, meanwhile, was convalescing in a local hospital after an appendicitis operation. When the announcement was made in the *Pine Bluff Commercial*, Critz told *Commercial* reporter Bill Hamner that Ferguson would "probably be retained."

Ferguson did stay and was named dean of men and director of student work to go along with his teaching position on the history faculty.

From a distance, Ferguson watched the public adulation of Sherman with a mixture of scorn and bemusement. Boosters, with the approval of Critz, set up contribution lists to raise money to subsidize the expected influx of football talent. Business men and faculty alike were pressured into "voluntary" contributions. Even Ferguson silently signed up for $10 a month.

Shortly after Sherman's arrival, Critz devised a scheme to bring students – and particularly football players – to A&M that would have made P.T. Barnum proud. Critz, Sherman, assorted politicians, (including Monticello Mayor Virgil McCloy and State Senator William F. Norrell) along with members of the faculty and Chamber of Commerce would lead caravans of cars and buses all over southern Arkansas in a traveling pep rally and tent revival. They would preach the gospel of Boll Weevil football.

The caravans included two buses to carry the marching band and girls' drum corps. Faculty were "encouraged" to participate. As the caravan rolled into an unsuspecting community, a platform was constructed for Critz, Sherman and the other dignitaries while the band began making noise to draw a crowd. The length of each stop depended on the size of the community and the crowd.

Faculty members, including a few disgruntled Ph.D.'s, tooted tin whistles given to them by President Critz. When enough curious townspeople gathered to see what the fuss was about, Critz, Sherman and members of the girls' drum corps climbed on the platform where Critz began his sales pitch, mixing football with a hint of sex.

Raising his hands to quiet the crowd, Critz began speaking slowly and deliberately in his rich baritone. "Friends, I've been told," said a grinning Critz while turning to look at the shapely bare legs of the girls in the drum corps, "that it takes legs to win football games." Hugely satisfied with himself and at the laughter from his audience, Critz would launch into his sales pitch, asking for the community's support of the football program and Coach Sherman. And if they could see fit to send their biggest, fastest young men to Arkansas A&M, well, that would be just fine.

When Sherman finally spoke, he was brief and to the point. "Just watch us," he said. "We'll take 'em all."

The Great Depression of the 1930's had a dramatic impact on college athletics, particularly at smaller schools like Arkansas A&M. The widespread and prevailing poverty created itinerant athletes who moved from college to college looking for a square meal and a roof over their heads. In exchange, they played football or basketball with little thought to attending class, even if they knew what classes they were supposed to attend. It was easily done at small, rural colleges where eligibility rules were loosely enforced. Ferguson referred to these players as football thugs and tramp athletes.

In the fall of 1935, Sherman brought 40 of them to Arkansas A&M, including transfers from the College of the Ozarks and his old school, Henderson State. Some hadn't finished the eighth grade while others had changed schools so often they made no pretense of presenting credits to the college registrar. Several were admitted using a loophole that allowed anyone 21 or older to attend if they could pass a psychological examination. Some had to be helped through the exam, but as a professor who administered the test rationalized, "After all, football players aren't supposed to know anything."

Sherman liked his players tough. To Ferguson, he seemed to value toughness and rough play over football ability. Sherman's first team was a mixture of city toughs and backwoods roughnecks who despised each other almost as much as the other teams. This toxic mix was a recipe for disaster and Ferguson knew it.

The Boll Weevils began the 1935 season with three straight losses while being outscored 77-0. The town's biggest boosters were shocked. Many thought Sherman was the football savior who would lead the school and town to football glory. Spirits brightened the next week with a 28-0 win over Arkansas State but the happiness was short-lived. The Boll Weevils lost their next four to finish with one victory and seven defeats.

Critz resigned as president the following January due to ill health. He confided privately to Ferguson that the play of the football team would make anyone sick.

Marvin Bankston, head of the agriculture department, replaced Critz as president. Bankston didn't like the way the football program was being conducted but his political instincts told him not to rock the boat too soon.

The disastrous '35 season failed to dampen the spirits of the most ardent boosters, who redoubled their efforts to raise more cash to spend on football talent. The new recruits were even rougher than the previous year's crop. Two had to be sobered up for practices and games.

The steady flow of cash failed to yield any appreciable improvement. The '36 season ended with a 2-5 record and a rising swell of discontent among the team's supporters. When the season was over, Bankston put an end to the athletic slush fund, ending the organized subsidization of athletes at Arkansas A&M.

Since state funding was available for student labor, Ferguson proposed that the football players work at campus jobs for their tuition, room and board. The jobs would be cushy and require little work, but the players rejected the idea out of hand. "I'm not damn fool enough to win a game for a college that won't give you room and board," said one disgruntled player.

With no football scholarships, shrinking gate receipts and the steady departure of players, the 1937 season was a disaster, starting with a season-opening 111-0 loss to Northeast Center Junior College (now Louisiana-Monroe) that saw the Indians score 17 touchdowns. (It remains the worst defeat in school history. At the time, Northeast Center was virtually a minor league team for LSU, feeding talent to the Baton Rouge campus. Four of Northeast Center's players who had a hand in the 111-0 massacre went on to become All-Americans, three at LSU and one at Tulane.) Things got so bad that Sherman made most of the boys in his one-hour physical education class try out for the football team. When the season came to a merciful conclusion, the Boll Weevils were 1-5 and had been outscored 228-40.

The next spring, Bankston and Ferguson took a tour of Sorrells Hall, which for the previous three years had served as the football dormitory and was virtually off limits to the rest of the university. Bankston and Ferguson were shocked by what they found. The halls were littered with piles of broken liquor bottles, ankle-deep dirt and mounds of paper and trash. Walls had been knocked down to merge rooms together. Furniture was smashed, walls were covered with sexually explicit drawings and graffiti. A hideous odor came from several rooms where private toilets had been created by punching holes through the floor. One player had used a BB gun to shoot flies off the ceiling.

The destruction in the dormitory confirmed Ferguson's feelings about Sherman's players. Most were not typical of A&M students; they were hired guns and tramps who didn't belong on a college campus.

Shortly after the inspection, Sherman was fired, ending a three-year experiment that resulted in four wins, 17 losses and the near destruction of the football program.

Sentiment was growing to drop the sport.

CHAPTER 6

SUCKERED

Stewart Ferguson was happy in the life of a college professor. Since being fired as head football coach after the 1934 season, he had taken on more academic responsibilities. He was now head of the Department of Health and Physical Education as well as history professor, dean of men, and director of student work. He was spending his summers in Baton Rouge as a visiting professor at LSU working on a doctorate. As an educated bachelor on a college campus, Ferguson was enjoying the company of any number of attractive young graduate students. He was also developing a reputation in the academic community as an original thinker and was sought as a consultant and speaker.

Ferguson had been secretly delighted by Sherman's near destruction of the A&M football program. After all, if a coach with Sherman's credentials couldn't win there, maybe Ferguson wasn't such a bad coach after all.

The Sherman era had been a disaster and sentiment was mounting in town and on campus to discontinue football. The townspeople were disillusioned, angry, and weary from constantly being pressured for donations to support what many considered a band of football renegades. The sport that was supposed to make Monticello and Arkansas A&M famous had instead made them infamous.

Sherman's final season had been marked with dirty play to such an extent that even some A&M supporters cringed at the spectacle. "Why should we maintain a gang of thugs on the campus and advertise it to the state in football games?" asked one professor.

Not everyone agreed with that sentiment. The student editor of the 1938 *Boll Weevil* yearbook praised Sherman for "time and again representing Monticello with an unusually good team considering the material he had to build it from," then took a swipe at the administration. "We offer no apologies. We are proud of our team, our coach, and our college."

Thomas "Eddie Mac" McMillan, one of Sherman's physical education students who joined the football team in 1937 liked his coach. "People wrote some mighty bad things about him," McMillan remembered years later. "As for how he treated me, I couldn't have asked for a better man."

When Sherman was finally relieved of his coaching duties in the spring of 1938, President Bankston faced a difficult decision – drop football completely or try to start over with a new coach, no money and very little community support.

Bankston had played a little football himself at Arkansas A&M when it was still a high school and wanted to keep the sport. He made the announcement late in the spring term that A&M would play football in 1938. Now he had to find a coach.

Several names were presented to the Board of Trustees, including Ouachita Coach W.I. "Bill" Walton, Duke Wells of Henderson State, J. O. Plummer of Monticello High School, and Allen Dunnaway of Pine Bluff High.

Bankston wasn't interested in any of them. If football was going to be played at Arkansas A&M, the school would run the program, not the boosters. Critz had essentially ceded control of the football program to a few influential townspeople who backed Sherman. Those days were over. Bankston wanted someone who would strike a balance between athletics and academics. He wanted Stewart Ferguson.

Bankston's view of college athletics was ambivalent at best. A few months earlier he had publicly called for the dissolution of the Arkansas Intercollegiate Athletic Association, saying the organization had "served its purpose." At the time the AIAA consisted of six public four-year colleges (Arkansas A&M, Arkansas Tech in Russellville, Arkansas State in Jonesboro, Magnolia A&M, Arkansas State Teachers College in Conway, Henderson State Teachers College in Arkadelphia), two private colleges (Ouachita Baptist College in Arkadelphia, Hendrix College in Conway) and Little Rock Junior College.

"I am not satisfied with the present conference and I do not believe anyone else is," Bankston told the *Arkansas Gazette.*

The AIAA was indeed suffering from a credibility problem. Ouachita had been barred from playing any of the other member schools after being disqualified by the North Central Association. In 1937, Little Rock JC made no attempt to carry out an intercollegiate sports schedule, Magnolia A&M dropped football for the season for lack of players and Arkansas A&M's schedule was limited to six games, none after November 5. Sherman had gone so far as to make a public plea in the November 8 *Gazette* for any school interested in playing a game "Friday and a week from Friday."

A day after Bankston's interview in the *Gazette,* Arkansas State announced its decision to leave the AIAA although the Indians would still play against AIAA schools. ASU President Herbert Schwartz outlined plans for an alternative conference consisting of ASU, Arkansas A&M and Magnolia A&M. The three schools would play each other twice a year on a home-and-home basis with no admission charge. Game day would become an "athletic carnival with other sports before and after the game. The conference has been formed in an effort to foster a better relationship between the three schools," said Schwartz. According to the *Gazette* story, "The sports carnivals will continue for two days. Band and orchestra competition will be a feature. Schwartz estimated that 60 or more students from each institution would take part in the athletic events."

This three-team conference lasted one season. Arkansas A&M and ASU did play twice in 1938 but the experiment didn't last.

It was into this atmosphere that Bankston decided Ferguson could lend stability to Arkansas A&M's football program. Bankston was subtle in his pursuit, dropping hints that Ferguson either wouldn't take or ignored completely. Finally, Bankston broached the subject directly. Would Ferguson consider taking over as head football coach?

Ferguson was aghast. He was enjoying himself too much and had learned over the three previous years that there were better ways to earn a living than coaching. A professor doesn't take weekly examinations before thousands of people who are sure they know more about his subject than he does, Ferguson told Bankston. Professors don't lose their jobs because of bad weather or a sprained ankle.

Ferguson would have none of it and avoided Bankston until it was time to leave for LSU on June 1. Ferguson was looking forward to another summer in Baton Rouge and his thoughts were on the attractive, south Louisiana school teachers who roamed the LSU campus. Football could go to hell.

A week after arriving in Baton Rouge, Ferguson received a letter from Bankston that included a contract for the football coaching job. Ferguson returned the unsigned contract that afternoon with a strongly worded letter indicating that if he took the job, both he and Bankston would be out of work within the year.

"You can't slap thousands of people in the face with a dead herring and make them like it," Ferguson added in a postscript.

Bankston wouldn't give up. He sent Ferguson a letter that basically ignored Ferguson's initial refusal and informed him that he was indeed the coach. Ferguson again refused, asking Bankston "why he was so determined to start chopping cotton again."

Three days later, the phone rang in Ferguson's apartment. It was Bankston calling to tell him he was the Arkansas A&M football coach and had been for several days. Ferguson was still yelling "No" when Bankston hung up.

Desperate to avoid returning to what he considered a career-killing job, Ferguson wrote his old friend, Scott Brame, principal at Bolton High in Alexandria, to see if he had any openings. Brame sent Ferguson a contract the next day and Ferguson sent his formal resignation to Monticello.

Bankston called the next day and asked Ferguson not to sign the contract. He was sending C. C. Smith, his smooth-talking business manager, to Baton Rouge the next morning.

Smith's persuasive powers were legend at A&M and Ferguson knew he had to be careful dealing with his old friend. Smith had always taken care of Ferguson, wiring money all over the country to help him out of jams when he overspent on vacations in Chicago, Memphis, Los Angeles, and San Antonio.

Smith took Ferguson to lunch on the LSU campus and told him he agreed with his decision not to coach again and both men laughed at Bankston for believing Ferguson might give in and take the job. "I'm pretty much of a fool," said Ferguson, "but even fools don't put their necks against buzz saws."

After lunch, Smith and Ferguson walked to the Greek Theatre to discuss Ferguson's future. In the shade of a massive live oak dripping with Spanish moss, Ferguson was a little drowsy on a full stomach and Smith's next comment took him by surprise.

"Coach," Smith began (he always referred to Ferguson as coach), "we've decided to give you a raise of $50 a month for next year. Do you think that's enough?"

Ferguson thanked Smith, then stopped short. "Oh, I know," said Ferguson. "You're trying to get me to coach again. No, you can't pay me enough to coach."

Smith assured Ferguson there would not be one word in his contract about coaching.

"Well, that's different," Ferguson said. "I just thought you were trying to get me to coach again."

Ferguson thanked Smith for the raise. Smith again assured Ferguson that coaching was not to be part of his job, then moved in for the kill. "Mr. Bankston and I both feel you deserve the raise," said Smith. "Whenever we're in a pinch, you're always the first to help out. You can do anything. I'd like to see the job that you couldn't handle. You're just a damn good man."

Ferguson was puffing up like a balloon.

"Now," Smith continued, "let's suppose Dean Hutchinson quits. Who do you think could take over his work? And you'd do a good job at it. Now let's say for fun that we can't find a coach for next year. You'd help out, I'm sure."

Ferguson would not coach and if Bankston and Smith couldn't find one, he'd find one for them.

"We can find one," said Smith, "but what can we find? Some dumb bruiser who'll ruin the boys and the college. I'd rather we didn't have a coach than one like that. Come to think of it, I don't think we better have a coach at all."

"You mean you're going to cut out football?" Ferguson asked.

No, Arkansas A&M would play football, said Smith. "And, I believe that if you are around to sorta help out the boys when they get in trouble that everything will work out all right."

"I damn sure won't do any coaching," Ferguson responded.

Smith assured him he was not asking him to coach. "I was just hinting that you might help the boys out when they get in trouble."

Ferguson was hooked. "Of course, you know I'll do that," he said. "I might even be willing to give them ideas once in a while, but of course, I won't coach."

Smith, Bankston and Ferguson would sit on the bench during games to keep the boys from fighting and maybe go to practice from time to time. Ferguson would make out the schedules and buy the equipment.

"That's the stuff," said Smith. "We knew we could depend on you. And, remember, Coach, you can tell the players anything you want to. In fact, you can do just about anything you damn please. No one's going to interfere with you and your ideas even if you are not the coach."

Who would take the blame for losses, Ferguson wondered.

"President Bankston and I are not going to let them blame you even if we lose every game for three years," Smith said. "Now, when can we expect you back to start work?"

Ferguson wanted the particulars on paper. Smith reached in his pocket, took out a cancelled envelope and started writing. Ferguson was not being hired to coach, didn't have to win a game for three years and could do anything he pleased in the athletic program. It was a contract unique in the annals of college athletics.

Later, after Smith had left, Ferguson pondered the agreement. What was the difference, he thought, between coaching and helping the boys out, giving them ideas, attending practices, and sitting on the bench during games?

He'd been suckered and he knew it. Stewart Ferguson was a coach again.

CHAPTER 7

BACK IN THE FIRE

Local response ranged from anger to apathy at the news that Stewart Ferguson was once again the head football coach at Arkansas A&M. Ferguson didn't care. He had decided to enjoy his summer at LSU and forget about football until it was time to call the first practice.

Why should Ferguson worry? He possessed the closest thing to an ironclad contract any coach had ever had. He didn't have to win a game for three years. He could do anything he wanted in the athletic department. He could coach if he felt like it, or not coach if he didn't feel like it. He would do no recruiting. The school's dismal football record, a lack of cash to give recruits, and his own sullied coaching reputation weren't going to attract much football talent to A&M.

The first day of practice for the 1938 season yielded a squad small in numbers, size and talent, mostly undersized country boys from the small rural high schools scattered throughout the region. Ferguson had hoped to persuade two of the best players from Monticello High School to join the team, but the only recruit turned out to be a girl cheerleader.

Ferguson's primary goal prior to the start of the '38 season was to wrest control of the football program from local boosters, even if it meant cutting ties with the community. When a three-member committee from the Chamber of Commerce came to see Ferguson shortly after practice began, Ferguson let the committee know who was in charge.

After an exchange of uncomfortable pleasantries, the committee spokesman, a vocal opponent of Ferguson in the past, spoke up. Ferguson could be sure, he drawled, that the Chamber of Commerce only wanted to help promote the athletics program and perhaps make Ferguson a better coach in the process. As he spoke, Ferguson remembered every slight, every criticism, every rebuke he had endured from his one season as coach of the Boll Weevils. When the spokesman finished, he weakly offered Ferguson his hand and invited him to join the Chamber.

Ferguson gave him a withering stare. "The only cooperation I've ever had from any of you was when you all joined together in kicking me out of a job," he reminded them. He went on to say that if they wanted to run the football team, he should be allowed to run their businesses, which in his opinion needed plenty of improvement.

One of the committee reminded Ferguson that he was a public employee working for the taxpayers while another thought it might be a good idea to rid the college of ungrateful and uncooperative imbeciles. Ferguson responded that the only imbeciles he knew were in the Chamber of Commerce. With that, the committee stomped out.

Ferguson had made a clean break and he knew it. He would never again have any support from downtown boosters, which was just the way he wanted it. If they didn't support the program, they would not be meddling in its operation.

Ferguson's confrontation with the Chamber was as much about

President Bankston as it was about himself and the football team. Bankston was receiving heat for hiring Ferguson and Ferguson wanted to deflect the criticism away from his boss, a man he both liked and respected.

As the '38 season drew near, Ferguson tried to piece together a football team from the previous season's holdovers and the few new players he had managed to attract. Four veterans from Sherman's last team joined the squad – guards Coy Brown and Eddie McMillan, who played in the line at a whopping 5-7 and 134 pounds, halfback Carleton Spears, and end Stanley Cheshier.

Most of the players had no knowledge of Ferguson's previous coaching success in South Dakota and Louisiana. They saw him as a soft-spoken, slightly built history teacher who neither talked nor acted like any coach they had ever known. He was certainly not Bo Sherman. From the first day of practice, Sherman ran his players until they vomited or fell out, unable to take another step. Ferguson rarely pushed them to their physical limits. Sherman believed in constant scrimmaging but under Ferguson, the Weevils rarely scrimmaged, and when they did, the contact was light.

When the players ventured downtown, the locals bashed Ferguson at every opportunity. The student body and many of the faculty were convinced that Bankston had decided to scrap the football program and had brought Ferguson back to do the job.

The first game of the '38 season was scheduled for September 23 against Mississippi State Teachers College (later the University of Southern Mississippi) in Hattiesburg. Ferguson's best player was a freshman end from Pine Bluff named Tom Curry.

The night before the game, Ferguson called his team together at their hotel. He knew his boys were outmanned but he hoped to avoid a shutout. Scoring, even if just once, against this Mississippi team would be a huge confidence boost for his players, and the best shot to score was Tom Curry. As Ferguson explained how Curry could get free for a long touchdown pass, a Western Union courier knocked on the door.

Ferguson quickly opened the wire, thinking it was from fans wishing his team well. The telegram read "Tom Curry ineligible. Do not play him." The faculty athletic committee was up to its old tricks. Ferguson wondered how the same committee that, under Bo Sherman, would have let Capone or Dillinger play, didn't hesitate to make Ferguson's best player ineligible.

Without Curry, the Boll Weevils had no chance. Ferguson sat forlornly on the bench as the Mississippi team rolled to a 39-0 victory, not as lopsided as he had feared but an indicator that he and his team were in for a long season. Ferguson was right. The Weevils began the year by suffering five straight shutouts and were outscored 238-26 while compiling a winless 0-9 record.

When the season was over, Ferguson knew drastic changes had to be made to keep the football program afloat. He told Bankston and Smith he wanted to cancel most, if not all, of Arkansas A&M's home games and schedule games across the country that would provide cash guarantees. Smith was skeptical. "Coach, I've been involved in athletics all my life," he said. "If you can make money at this, you'll have to show me." Ferguson insisted he could, and with the blessing of Bankston and Smith, sent letters to colleges and universities across the country. Most of the letters went to coaches Ferguson had met while teaching summer school at LSU. Many of those same coaches were now taking correspondence courses taught by Ferguson and were eager to accommodate their instructor. To Ferguson's delight, he received several positive responses, including game contracts. Ferguson brought the contracts to Smith, who added up the guarantees, compared them to expenses, then smiled. "By God, you can make money, can't you," Smith exclaimed.

Ferguson arranged a 10-game schedule in 1939 that would take his team from Pennsylvania to Texas and points in between with only two home games. Only one Arkansas opponent – Hendrix – remained on the schedule.

The lack of home games wasn't based solely on economics; it was also Ferguson's way of thumbing his nose at the fans in Monticello, but not long after the schedule was finalized, he began to have second thoughts. How stupid was it, he reasoned, to schedule games with teams that could likely "kick his players through the goal posts."

In truth, as Ferguson later admitted, he had scheduled the games " most likely for the hell of it." Unknowingly, he had planted the seeds for the strangest football team ever assembled.

CHAPTER 8

FOOTBALL FOR FUN

The schedule facing the Arkansas A&M football team in 1939 was a daunting one:

Sept. 15	Louisiana Tech	at Ruston, Louisiana
Sept. 30	St. Joseph's	at Philadelphia, Pennsylvania
Oct. 6	Morris Harvey	at Charleston, West Virginia
Oct. 14	Daniel Baker	at Odessa, Texas
Oct. 20	Louisiana College	at Monticello
Nov. 4	Missouri School of Mines	at Rolla, Missouri
Nov. 11	John Carroll	at Cleveland, Ohio
Nov. 17	Northwest Mississippi JC	at Monticello
Nov. 24	Hendrix	at Conway, Arkansas
Nov. 30	Missouri State Teachers	at Springfield, Missouri

It was an impossible challenge. Cross country travel in the 1930's was tedious, time-consuming and sometimes dangerous. There were no interstate highways and many of the main roads were still covered in gravel. The wear and tear of travel over poor roads on a battered school bus and the quality of the opponents meant more losing. Ferguson knew it, which is why he spent most of that summer applying for jobs all over the country. With each rejection, he became more resigned to his fate. He was about to coach a team that would take awful beatings each week, but at least they might have some fun.

Shortly before Ferguson arranged the '39 schedule, he sat down with Bankston and Smith and created a set of 10 rules which would govern the football program with the focus on making the sport fun for the players. The rules were:

1. Football is conducted according to the best principles and theory of both general education and physical education.
2. The game is played for the fun in it.
3. All high-pressure policies and procedures will be eliminated.
4. Football is made more educational through experimental approaches, player responsibility, and travel.
5. Intersectional schedules are played for the promotion of a wide range of contacts with other teams and student bodies.
6. Original, unique, and non-standardized formations, plays, and tactics are used to emphasize player thinking and initiative.
7. Liberal and democratic policies are used with as much responsibility as possible placed upon the players.
8. No players are subsidized.
9. Clean, courteous, and sportsmanlike play is stressed constantly.
10. The attitudes, welfare, and interests of the players are always placed above the outcome of the game.

Ferguson's principles represented a radical departure from conventional thinking in college athletics. Games were played to win, not for the enjoyment of the players. Lofty ideals like sportsmanship received lip service from coaches and administrators, but no coach was ever fired because his players weren't good sports.

The benefits, Ferguson believed, would be in the education his players received outside the traditional classroom setting and away from the isolated and insular environment of rural southeast Arkansas. His players would be exposed to different people, cultures and ideas that would challenge their preconceived notions and prejudices. They would come back from their travels broadened intellectually in ways their fellow students would never be.

When Ferguson returned to Monticello in August after another summer at LSU, he set about changing the A&M football program. The first order of business was to purchase new uniforms. He chose a gaudy combination of bright yellow jerseys with green numerals and shoulder stripes, ignoring the traditional college colors of green and white. Word around Monticello was that yellow was a perfect color for Ferguson's teams.

Ferguson's private life was also undergoing a major change. The previous summer, he had received a letter from 18-year-old Edna McAdam, a newly-minted high school graduate from Hot Springs, South Dakota. McAdam was searching for someplace to attend college and the Hot Springs superintendent was acquainted with Ferguson, knew he was head of the A&M student work program, and thought he could help.

Ferguson hired McAdam sight unseen to be his personal secretary and the two began a secret courtship. By 1939, they were living together, creating a local scandal made worse by their 20-year age difference. They would be married a year later, but in the meantime, Ferguson would have to rein in his well-earned reputation as a ladies man, at least in Monticello.

Practice for the '39 season was scheduled to begin a week before students registered for classes, but when the only player to report turned out to be Ferguson's student assistant in physical education, he wisely set the next practice to coincide with registration day.

That left eight days to prepare for the opener with first-time opponent Louisiana Tech, one of the region's toughest teams.

A dozen players reported for the first practice, most who fancied themselves as backs, not linemen. Ferguson tried to entice more players by promising that everyone who came out for the team would get to travel to Ruston, Louisiana for the first game. Gradually, more players of questionable ability joined the team, but the Weevils were still woefully short on talent.

The Monday of game week dawned bright and sunny and Ferguson was desperate. He found himself pacing the football field lost in thought, wondering how his rag tag collection of players would survive the brutal schedule he had conceived.

As Ferguson continued to wander aimlessly around the field, he was approached by two boys who had just arrived from Little Rock. Terry Field was over six feet tall, handsome and athletic, the kind of athlete who made coaches drool. His companion was more than a half foot shorter, couldn't weigh more than 130 pounds thought Ferguson, and answered to the name Annie.

The boys wanted to play football if Ferguson would agree to pay their board, room, tuition and laundry. Ferguson told them the best he could do was pay for their travel, then turned to walk away.

"Hey," said Field. "I guess we'll stay."

The smaller player had a question. "Do we have to practice this afternoon?" Ferguson was so grateful to have Field that he told them both no. He would see them at practice the next afternoon.

Watching Field warm up the next day gave Ferguson a warm feeling. The boy was big, smart and fast. The smaller boy mostly fooled around, then sauntered over to Ferguson to ask him what position he wanted him to play.

"The same as you played at Little Rock," said Ferguson.

"Yeah," said the boy, "but I was just a cheerleader!"

Ferguson laughed at what he thought was a joke and walked

over to Field. "That kid's a clown," he said.

"Sure," said Field, "and he's just a cheerleader, too. The coach at Little Rock wouldn't let him come out for the team. Afraid he'd get killed."

Field wasn't kidding. James "Annie" Robinson had been a cheerleader at Little Rock High School. He was also a versatile and accomplished athlete with a strong right arm who managed to play quarterback for the Little Rock junior varsity team before his coach handed him a megaphone and told him someone his size would be better suited for cheerleading. From then on, Robinson was known as "Annie" thanks to the good-natured taunts of his former teammates.

Robinson refused to let his slight stature or his nickname become an obstacle to his athletic dreams. He entered amateur boxing matches, winning several bouts. He pitched for local baseball teams, was a high-scoring forward on three independent basketball teams, and in his spare time, peddled popcorn for the Arkansas Travelers, Little Rock's minor league baseball team.

Robinson would be Ferguson's quarterback.

The rest of the starters, depending on the whim of the players, included left end Robert Maskell of Booneville, left tackle Paul Stegall of Monticello, left guard, captain and unofficial team spokesman Coy Brown of Levy, center Collier Jordan of Vernon, Ala., right guard Thomas Hooker of Pine Bluff, right tackle Terry Field of Little Rock, right end Stanley Cheshier of Monticello, left halfback Tunis Bishop of Little Rock, right halfback Boyd Arnold of Bearden, and fullback and co-captain Carleton Spears of Clarendon. Top reserves included guard John Arnold (no relation to Boyd), halfback Buell Bishop (brother of Tunis), and halfback Pete Cheshier (brother of Stanley).

The team was not without talent. Stanley Cheshier was an accomplished pass receiver and Boyd Arnold had the squad's only legitimate college football credentials, having earned second team All-Border Conference honors in 1937 at the Texas School of Mines (later the University of Texas at El Paso). By the time Arnold transferred to A&M, his legend had grown to the point that he was listed as an AP Little All-American in the school yearbook, *The Boll Weevil*. Arnold apparently did nothing to dispel the myth. Overall, the backs and linemen were quick, but a lack of size at all positions left the Boll Weevils vulnerable to bigger, stronger opponents. Unfortunately, that description fit every team on the '39 schedule.

The day before the season opener, Ferguson was in a panic. His new uniforms and equipment hadn't arrived. Several calls to area high schools produced polite rejections. To make matters worse, the athletic committee was up to its old tricks. The committee had declared most of the team academically ineligible. Ferguson was so angry he retreated to the nearest men's restroom and held down the flush handle to drown out a steady barrage of cursing.

If that's the way those pinheads wanted it, then Ferguson would make them deal with the consequences. The angry coach found the committee chairman and told him if his players' eligibility was not restored immediately, then the committee would take the heat for cancelling the game and paying a sizable fee for the forfeit. Ferguson then found Bankston and told him about the committee's attempts to scuttle his football team.

Bankston called the committee together and reminded them that it was their job to "carry out the athletic program rather than kill it." After much throat clearing and mumbling, the committee cited an error in paperwork for the problem. Of course the boys could play. It was all a misunderstanding.

Reprieve in hand, Ferguson hurried to find his team and hustled them onto the bus for a quick getaway before the committee changed its mind. When the Boll Weevils arrived in Ruston Friday afternoon, Ferguson found the only hotel big enough to house his team, but there was another problem. The manager didn't like football players and wasn't about to let them stay in his hotel. Ferguson escorted the man outside to take a look at his collection of small, scrawny farm boys and the manager, either out of pity or shock, relented and let them stay.

Ferguson persuaded Tech officials to let his team borrow their road uniforms and just enough helmets and pads to outfit his squad, then settled in for a pleasant evening at the hotel. Despite the mayhem and confusion surrounding preparations for the game, Ferguson had managed to arrange for some female companionship, booking a room next to his for an attractive young high school teacher he had met over the summer at LSU.

The next morning, after getting his ankles and knee taped, Eddie McMillan ventured into the hallway and headed back to his room. He was clad in a jock strap and nothing else, save the athletic tape on his ankles and knee. As he stepped into the hallway he was hugged by an attractive young woman who happened to be his former teacher at Parkdale High School and a friend of McMillan's sister. As McMillan and his former teacher talked, a scowling Ferguson appeared, tapped his player on the shoulder and told him to get dressed, then escorted McMillan's former teacher to her room.

McMillan was already aware of Ferguson's philandering. Weeks earlier, while taking summer classes at A&M, McMillan and a friend were sitting on the balcony at the end of their dormitory, drinking beer and enjoying the warm summer evening. Their reverie was interrupted when they spotted Ferguson strolling down the sidewalk with a young woman on his arm. Ferguson led his companion into the empty dorm next to McMillan's. "They went into one of the rooms we could see into," remembered McMillan. "He was trying to get her to have sex with him. The window was open and we could hear everything."

That evening, when the boys were dressed and ready, Ferguson stood before them and asked for quiet. As he looked at his team, the old Stewart Ferguson bubbled to the surface, the combative, competitive, win-at-all-costs coach he had been in South Dakota. He told them to "give their all for their college, their parents, their sisters, brothers, and the girls they intend to marry." Speaking slowly and allowing his eyes to mist over for dramatic effect, he told them the game they were about to play would be with them for the rest of their lives. Why, Ferguson would give years of his own life for a chance to be in their shoes. As the words rushed out, Ferguson thought to himself that he wouldn't set foot on that field for a year's salary.

So much for playing the game for fun. In one brief pep talk, Ferguson had broken at least four of the 10 lofty ideals he had conceived to govern the Arkansas A&M football program.

As his fired up team burst through the dressing room doors and raced to the field, Ferguson was already feeling remorseful. He had done the worst thing a coach could do. He had given his team hope that it could win and set his players up for morale-shattering failure. As he watched his boys, he realized he hadn't even taught them how to warm up properly.

The game was delayed 30 minutes by a severe electrical storm, an omen of what was about to occur. When the game finally began, it went about as Ferguson had expected. Louisiana Tech was too big, too deep, and too talented for the Boll Weevils. Tech Coach Ray Davis emptied his bench, using his entire squad to grind down the outmanned Weevils. The only bright spot was the play of Annie Robinson, who completed several long passes in the second half, mostly out of desperation to avoid being tackled by one of the Bulldogs' huge linemen.

The 32-0 defeat left the Boll Weevils battered physically. A quick inventory revealed two broken noses, several sprained ankles, a twisted knee, and assorted bumps and bruises. Worse were the looks on the players' faces. Gone were the expressions of eager anticipation Ferguson had seen before the game, replaced with disappointment and disillusionment. They had believed their coach when he said they could win.

The bus ride home was miserable. Ferguson was in a mental and emotional fog. He had prostituted his high ideals one more time and his players had paid the price. Ferguson spent most of the three hour ride mentally whipping himself. As he stared out the bus window into the darkness, Ferguson knew he had to make a fundamental change to the way he ran the football program. The sport, he believed, had much to offer, but only if the boys actually had fun playing the game. He thought about the next two opponents – St. Joseph's College in Philadelphia and Morris-Harvey College in Charleston, West Virginia. His team would be overmatched in each contest. He felt guilty about accepting the game guarantees if his team couldn't put up a presentable effort.

As he thought about the folly of taking his team across the country to absorb beating after beating, Ferguson had an idea. A completely original idea. His players were going to have fun playing the game, by God. He would insist on it. And the fans were going to have fun watching his players have fun. The Arkansas A&M football team would play the game as a comedy in four acts.

Stewart Ferguson was through coaching football to win. He would look for the good in the game and if that meant turning a serious sport into a farce, so be it. Now if he could just convince his players to go along.

CHAPTER 9

GRIDIRON CLOWNS

It was an absurd idea.

The Boll Weevils knew their coach was eccentric, but now some of the boys thought he'd slipped over the edge. The day after the loss at Louisiana Tech, Ferguson called his team together before practice. As he explained his idea to turn football into comedy, the players looked back, slack-jawed.

Football was full of opportunities to be funny and have fun, Ferguson told them. They would change the game in a fundamental way. They would be pioneers, turning football from drudgery to joy. As Ferguson became more animated, one of the more skeptical players interrupted.

Exactly how were they supposed to have fun and be funny playing football?

The boys weren't great players; they knew that. But they were competitive athletes who had been taught from childhood that the object of any game was to win. What in hell did their coach have in mind?

Ferguson wasn't feeling funny at the moment. In fact, he was angry that his players weren't buying in to his idea. He would show them what he meant on the practice field. After dividing the squad into two teams, Ferguson inserted himself into the backfield at halfback. He managed a few pratfalls in a feeble attempt to draw laughs, but his players just stared and Ferguson felt foolish.

"You boys had better start playing football for fun, by golly, or you'd better start playing football at some other college," he hissed, then told them to finish practice by playing touch football. Ferguson retreated to the dressing room and sat on a bench with his head in his hands. Should he finish the season, or just disappear to an island somewhere, he wondered. Ferguson stayed in the dressing room for an hour, then returned to the practice field where his players were engaged in one of the wildest games of touch football he'd ever witnessed. Laterals flew across the field with the ball rarely staying in one player's hands for more than a few seconds. It looked like a Chinese fire drill, Ferguson thought, but he was mesmerized. You can't coach boys to have fun or be funny, he realized. They have to find it on their own.

From then on, practices would consist mostly of touch football games with three to 12 on a side. All blocking and tackling drills were eliminated because they weren't fun. The touch football games were an exercise in democracy. The boy who thought up plays the fastest became the quarterback until someone else did it faster. The games and practices lasted as long as the players were having fun and no one kept score.

The Boll Weevils had 16 days between their opener at Louisiana Tech and their next game against St. Joseph's. Ferguson reminded the boys to eat, drink and have fun because they were going to get the hell kicked out of them in Philadelphia. The players just laughed. They were too excited about the upcoming trip to think about their next opponent.

The Weevils would make the trip in an old, battered green and white Chevrolet bus that struggled on steep grades and topped out at 50 miles an hour. Alvin Beverburg, a tall, thin, high-strung sophomore, was the driver. Beverburg had never driven in traffic or over hills steeper than the gentle rises that passed for hills in southeast Arkansas, but he would soon be asked to navigate the Appalachian Mountains and the streets of Philadelphia and New York City.

The new uniforms had arrived and the boys were antsy to begin the biggest adventure of their lives, a 15-day road trip that would take them more than 2,600 miles to Pennsylvania, New York, and West Virginia before returning to Monticello.

Early on the morning of September 26, 1939, Ferguson and 22 green, unsophisticated and excited boys boarded the bus. Ferguson had $300 travel money in his pocket and the promise of two game guarantee checks. He would be the boys' mother, father, coach and tour guide.

As the bus pulled away from campus, Ferguson gripped the $300 and thought of all the things that could go wrong. The boys chattered excitedly as the bus rumbled and rattled its way north over a rough gravel road toward Pine Bluff.

The miles passed and the players got quiet as they stared out the windows at the passing cotton fields ready for harvest. Sweat stained their shirts by the time they stopped for lunch in Forrest City, then it was on across the Mississippi River bridge at Memphis before stopping for supper in Jackson, Tennessee.

As darkness fell and the bus rolled toward Nashville and a waiting hotel, Ferguson surveyed his players. Directly behind him was Coy Brown, the starting left guard, a homely, sleepy-eyed boy with a perpetual smile on his face. Ferguson wasn't sure how smart the boy was, but thought that as long as he had a chaw of tobacco and a place to spit, he'd be happy. Brown may have appeared to be on the verge of falling asleep in mid-sentence, partly due to an eye condition that caused him to cock his head back to look someone in the eye, but he was a popular student, editor of the campus newspaper and president of the lettermen's club.

Seated next to Brown was wise-cracking halfback Tunis Bishop, just 18 and full of youthful bravado. Across the aisle was John Strange, a guard with a shock of red hair, crossed eyes and a squeaky voice. Strange had a penchant for straggling at every rest stop and Ferguson assigned two players to make sure he didn't miss the bus.

Close by was J.P. Leveritt, part-time player, part-time assistant coach, and full-time trainer, who treated the boys' bumps and bruises and inserted himself into games when needed. Leveritt was handsome, curly-headed and blessed with a muscular build created by a heavy regimen of weight lifting. He had been sickly as a child, diagnosed with a heart condition at 7 and unable to gain weight well into his teens. Determined to overcome his physical frailties, Leveritt bought a Charles Atlas course, became a dedicated weight lifter and built himself into a chiseled physical specimen.

As a football player, Leveritt was ahead of his time. Coaches in the 1930's and '40's had strict rules against weight training. They didn't want their players muscle-bound. Leveritt provided a striking argument to the foolishness of that idea. He was a lithe athlete with amazing flexibility and the balance of an accomplished acrobat. Leveritt was a self-taught gymnast with Olympic-class skills who could walk on his hands, do back flips and handsprings with ease. He was the best athlete on the squad and a devout Christian, but up to that point, had seen little action. Ferguson thought the muscular Leveritt didn't like physical contact.

A few rows back sat "The Preacher," 38-year-old tackle James Sewell, just one year younger than Ferguson and an ordained Methodist minister who conducted weekly services for the team. Next to him was Collier Jordan, a country boy from Alabama who doubled as the team barber. There was halfback and co-captain Carleton Spears, the handsome senior class president and mature beyond his years; guard and blocking back Eddie McMillan, who tried too hard to be smooth and became a magnet for trouble; and Loy Perry, who Ferguson fancied as something of a momma's boy.

The Little Rock boys, Annie Robinson and Terry Field, were a little more worldly than their country teammates. Robinson was a cocksure athlete whose confidence bordered on arrogance while Field had a well-earned reputation for being able to talk anybody into anything.

They were a good group of boys, Ferguson thought. Most were polite and almost all were deeply religious, although their language was sometimes unsuitable for a church. Ferguson rarely told them how to behave and had few, if any, rules regarding training or conduct. He treated them like men and allowed them the freedom to speak their minds. If tempers occasionally flared, he let the boys settle their differences.

After a night in a nondescript Nashville hotel, the Weevils were off early the next morning, headed east toward the Great Smoky Mountains. Progress was slow as the old bus wheezed and coughed its way up and down the hilly terrain. Ferguson had serious doubts about reaching their destination and the boys were growing irritable at the slow progress.

When the bus reached Cookeville, Ferguson directed Beverburg to drive to the campus of Tennessee Tech. He wanted his players to stretch their legs and loosen up on Tech's field. As the Boll Weevils kicked and tossed a ball around, two Tennessee Tech coaches watched from a distance, then approached Ferguson. "You mean to tell me that this is a college team," one of the coaches asked.

"Sure, and we're playing 10 tough games this fall," Ferguson answered.

"Maybe so," said the other coach, "but I'd like to see your team try to play Cookeville High School. I guess you must have a very fast team."

The Tech coaches peppered Ferguson with questions. What kind of offense did he use? Ferguson had no idea. In fact, he hadn't given it much thought, so he lied. "We're springing a surprise formation in Philadelphia and I'd rather not tell just what it is at present." It was a response Ferguson would use over and over with sportswriters and coaches as his team traveled the country.

"Well, I must say you are covering up plenty," said one of the coaches. "I haven't seen your team show a damn thing since they came on the field. If you have anything at all, you sure as hell have me fooled."

"That's just how we fool 'em all," Ferguson said as he herded his team back on the bus and out of Cookeville. The Weevils reached Marion, Virginia by nightfall, just in time to take the bus to a mechanic, who replaced the faulty transmission. The next day brought more mechanical problems. After a brief stop in Lexington to work out at the Virginia Military Institute, the Weevils made their way toward Charlottesville. As they neared the top of a fog-shrouded mountain separating Staunton and Charlottesville, the bus moved slower and slower before grinding to a halt. It simply didn't have enough power to crest the summit, so Ferguson and the players got out and pushed. As they did, it began to rain. By the time they reached the mountain top and climbed back on the bus, they were all soaked to the skin.

They still hadn't dried out when they reached Washington, D.C., in search of a tourist camp Ferguson had reserved, since all available hotels were booked. With Ferguson navigating, they drove around in circles for the better part of an hour until one of the players finally deciphered the directions and got them to their destination.

Before leaving Monticello, Ferguson had written President Roosevelt requesting an opportunity to bring his team to the White House and practice on the White House lawn. When he received no response, Ferguson dashed off a letter to Postmaster General James A. Farley, who graciously extended an invitation to the Boll Weevils to come by his office for a visit.

After a cold and mostly sleepless night in the unheated tourist cabins, Ferguson roused his boys and told them to clean up. They were going to meet a Washington dignitary. Farley proved to be a gracious host, possibly because he felt sorry for the bedraggled group of sleepy-eyed boys who were still wearing the clothes they had slept in. Farley spent an hour telling the boys stories that had them doubled over in laughter and even engaged in a nickel-matching contest with Robinson. Farley made them forget the travails of the previous three days and Ferguson thought the big man would have made a fine football coach.

After a tour of the capital which included Beverburg driving the bus up and down Pennsylvania Avenue three times, the Weevils were still smiling as they headed for Philadelphia.

****

Stewart Ferguson was a master of self-promotion. Before the Weevils left Monticello, he mailed news releases and player photographs to the Philadelphia press to drum up interest in his team. The reach of the media in 1939 was far less pervasive than it would become and the Philadelphia press appeared to know little about the Boll Weevils, or anything else west of the Allegheny Mountains.

A wire story that appeared in both the *Philadelphia Inquirer* and the *Philadelphia Record* prior to the game talked about the strong Arkansas team that would challenge St. Joseph's. Arkansas A&M was a wide open passing team that "tossed its way to victory in a majority of games" the previous year the papers said. Apparently news of the Boll Weevils' 0-9 record of 1938 hadn't reached Philadelphia. The story called Carleton Spears "the champion pass flipper of the Southwest" and went on to extol the talents of Boyd Arnold, elevating him to second team Little All-American.

When the Weevils arrived at the Hotel Normandie, Ferguson received a call from Hugh Kolbmann, a sportswriter for the *Inquirer*. Kolbmann wanted to know if the Boll Weevils were as wacky as most teams from Arkansas.

College football in Arkansas and the southwest had gained a national reputation for wide-open play. The University of Arkansas, under Fred Thomsen, had won the 1936 Southwest Conference championship while earning the title of "passingest team in the land." Sammy Baugh and Davey O'Brien had become passing legends at Texas Christian at a time when most football coaches viewed the forward pass with disdain.

Ferguson was eager to play along with Kolbmann's questions and the longer the two talked, the more Ferguson exaggerated. Why yes, his team was wacky and unconventional and his boys "didn't give a hoot" about winning. "We play for fun, that's all," he said. "We honestly don't care who wins."

Why do they only play for fun, Kolbmann wanted to know. "To make people laugh," said Ferguson.

"You mean you make people laugh at football games?" asked the incredulous reporter.

"Sure, you should see us," said Ferguson. "We'll trade a laugh for a touchdown anytime."

When Ferguson picked up copies of the *Inquirer*, *Press* and *Philadelphia Record* the next morning, he was pleased with the coverage. Amazingly, five of the *Record's* 12 football prognosticators picked the Boll Weevils to win. The *Inquirer's* banner headline read "All For Fun Team From Arkansas Is Hawks' Opponent." Kolbmann's story was full of the same errors that had appeared in the wire service reports and Ferguson was worried that he might have promised too much from his team. The boys weren't all that funny in their play – at least not yet – they just had fun playing.

Ferguson called the team together and showed them the story. Could they please put a little more effort into being funny at this afternoon's game so they wouldn't disappoint the paying customers and the press? But the boys were distracted. They had just met Davey O'Brien, the 1938 Heisman Trophy winner, and his teammates, the Philadelphia Eagles, who were also staying at the Normandie. The encounter with the pros had inspired the Weevils to play real football.

As the boys suited up for the game, Ferguson paced nervously outside the dressing room. Kolbmann approached. He wanted more information about the Weevils and their style of play.

"Who are your starters?" Kolbmann asked.

"I don't know," said Ferguson, pointing to his players. "Ask them."

"You mean you let the players themselves decide who plays?" asked Kolbmann. Ferguson nodded yes. In fact, all 22 players would play about the same amount so it really didn't matter who started.

As the game began, the Weevils surprised Ferguson and gave the fans a taste of what they'd read in the newspapers, returning the kickoff deep into St. Joseph's territory. As the ball carrier was about to be tackled, he deftly lateraled to a trailing teammate who nearly scored. Ferguson watched as his team lined up smartly and came off the ball in unison at the snap. Little Annie Robinson, who was calling the plays, promptly completed a pass, and even though the Weevils failed to score on their opening possession, they weren't embarrassing themselves as Ferguson had feared they might.

Robinson was having a great game and an even better time making up plays in the huddle. Once, with his team backed up to its own goal line and facing fourth down with eight yards to go, Robinson ignored conventional strategy and completed a 40-yard pass. When Robinson came off the field, Ferguson asked him about the decision. "I lost track of the downs," said Robinson. "Besides, it's too much trouble to keep up with what down it is."

Later in the game, with his team on the St. Joseph's three-yard line, Robinson retreated 15 yards before throwing a pass for a touchdown. It was one of two touchdowns scored by the Weevils in a 40-13 loss punctuated by wild formations and goofy plays featuring multiple laterals and lots of passing. It was all Ferguson had hoped for. In his postgame story for the *Inquirer*, Kolbmann described the Weevils offensive strategy as "the like of which has not been seen outside the recreation periods of the State Insane Asylum."

The fans had enjoyed the show and so had the players. Ferguson's boys had bought into his idea.

Ferguson was all smiles after the game until the St. Joseph's athletic director told him the $1,000 game guarantee was being held up by a court order. Arkansas A&M had failed to pay a bill for equipment purchased by boosters during Bo Sherman's last season. Ferguson was out of money and had to wire C. C. Smith for more, including an advance on his own salary.

With more cash in hand, thanks to Smith and Western Union, Ferguson treated the players to a big meal that evening. The next day, they were guests of the Philadelphia Eagles at their game with the Brooklyn Dodgers, riding to the stadium on the team bus, joining the players in their dressing room, and watching the game from the sideline.

Monday morning, Ferguson pointed Beverburg and the bus north. The Boll Weevils were going to the Big Apple.

CHAPTER 10

THE BIG APPLE

The bus was quiet as Beverburg drove through the Holland Tunnel, but the players broke into whoops and shouts as they reached Times Square. The boys hung their heads out the windows and craned their necks to look upward at the mammoth skyscrapers as they made their way through the concrete and steel canyons of Manhattan.

"Gawddamn," drawled a voice from the back of the bus. "Pa could put a lot 'a hay in that barn."

Beverburg committed several traffic violations as he maneuvered the bus around Times Square three times, but police, seeing "Arkansas A&M" emblazoned on the side, just laughed and waved him on. When the bus came to a stop, a professional tour guide hopped on to offer Ferguson and his team a quick tour of the heart of the city.

A trip to New York had been part of Ferguson's itinerary when he formulated the '39 schedule. He wanted his boys to see firsthand the greatest city in the world. He planned to spend a couple of days in the Big Apple and take his players to the New York World's Fair, but at the moment, his primary concern was finding a place to stay. The Weevils had left Philadelphia so quickly that he had forgotten to book hotel rooms.

Luckily the tour guide directed them to a friend who just happened to have an apartment house near Times Square. Ferguson rented four medium-sized apartments for two nights and the players scattered to claim beds, sofas and what other sleeping accommodations that might be available. Ferguson and Robert Maskell were reduced to sleeping in bath tubs, but sleep was the farthest thing from the players' minds.

The boys wanted to see the bright lights of New York. Ferguson wasn't worried about them finding trouble; none of them had any money. One of the players had left Arkansas with only a quarter. Ferguson handed out travelers' checks and cash, including some of his own money, so the boys could have a good time, but not too good.

The next day, Ferguson took his players to the World's Fair, a dazzling exposition in Queens 30 minutes from mid-town Manhattan, where they peeked into the future at a world that included superhighways, mass air travel and a new mode of communication called television. The boys were awestruck, as they were the next day when they surveyed New York from the top of the Empire State Building. Everything the players saw left them amazed by a city that resembled nothing they'd ever seen or experienced. They left New York with stars in their eyes, headed for West Virginia and a date with Morris Harvey College, but they weren't thinking about football.

They reached Charleston on Thursday, the day before their scheduled game on Friday, October 6. As the boys settled into their rooms for the night, Ferguson went to the hotel lobby and picked up copies of the *Charleston Daily Mail* and the *Charleston Gazette*. "Eagles Face Dazzling Air Attack in A. and M. Game" blared a headline in the *Gazette*. *"Looking for every trick known to the trade from a razzle-dazzle football machine from the southwest, Morris Harvey College's Golden Eagles will take on Arkansas A and M under Laidley Field's floodlights tonight at 8 o'clock in quest of their third victory of the season,"* the *Gazette's* story began. *"The Arkansas team, one of the many from that section of the nation that features a dazzling passing attack . . . A running attack? Yes, the Weevils have one of those things, too, but they seldom use it. They ran the ball only 17 times last week as compared to the average of 45 in college football today."*

Ferguson was delighted with the coverage. After just one game in their play-for-fun style, his Boll Weevils were becoming one of the most talked about football teams in the nation. A&M had even made the sports pages of the *New York Times*, which had a brief write-up about the loss to St. Joseph's.

The West Virginia press knew as little about Arkansas A&M as the Philadelphia papers, extolling the talents of Arnold and his "pass-flipping" sidekick, Spears. One account said Morris Harvey coach Jule Ward was "shaking in his boots while awaiting the Arkansas A. and M. Weevils."

Coach Stewart Ferguson's Weevils from the Ozarks (most of the boys had never seen the hills of northwest Arkansas, but no matter) *have an offense that looks more like touch-and-pass football. They soar over the field . . . and throw passes helter-skelter when they get the ball. Coach Ward is afraid that the Arkansans might get hot with their crazy plays and that his Eagles will blow sky high.*

As Ferguson read the papers, he turned to a man seated next to him. Unable to contain himself, Ferguson said, "I coach this bunch."

The man studied Ferguson for a moment. "Too bad," he said. "It just isn't right for Morris Harvey to bring in teams and then pound and slaughter them like they've done every game this year. I can't help but feel sorry for every team that comes here to play."

Ferguson wanted to know more. "Are they big?" he asked. (As usual, Ferguson had done no scouting.)

Yes, they were big, fast and rough.

"We're not afraid of 'em," Ferguson bragged, although he knew they should be.

"Yeah, that's what the last coach said, but he sure as hell was before the slaughter was over."

Ferguson wasn't sure if the man was kidding or not, so he visited with several Morris Harvey fans in the lobby. They all described the Eagles as having mountainous tackles and lightning-quick backs.

Ferguson shared the news with his players and cautioned them that there was a fine line between courage and foolishness. He was truly concerned for their health. The last thing he wanted was to limp back to Monticello with half his team too injured to play its next game.

His players didn't get the message. When 3,000 fans showed up the next night curious to see the unconventional team from Arkansas, the Boll Weevils were in a scrappy mood. They stopped the Eagles on downs at the 19-yard line on their first possession, and thanks to an interception by Spears and a fumble recovery by Strange, trailed by the respectable score of 7-0 at halftime.

Morris Harvey, which had already beaten its first two foes by decisive margins, wore down the Boll Weevils in the second half by using three platoons to keep fresh players in the game. 7-0 became 33-0, but the Weevils still managed to entertain the fans with an assortment of laterals which usually resulted in lost yardage.

The final score didn't matter to Ferguson and neither did the statistics (20 first downs to two, 422 yards total offense to nine). His team had showed grit, managed to keep the fans in their seats, and escaped their bigger, stronger foe with no serious injuries. It was time to go home.

Stewart Ferguson (back left) and the 1939 Wandering Weevils

The 1939 Weevils and the "Green Dawg" bus

STEWART FERGUSON

Coach

Coach Stewart Ferguson, ringmaster of Arkansas A&M's traveling football circus.

MARVIN S. BANKSTON
President

*Arkansas A&M President Marvin Bankston, the man who
turned the football program over to Stewart Ferguson.*

C. C. SMITH
Business Mgr.

*Arkansas A&M business manager C. C. Smith, the
man who negotiated Ferguson's no-win contract.*

1939 team captain Coy Brown

James "Annie" Robinson of Little Rock, quarterback
of the 1939 Wandering Weevils

Terry Field, who had a well-earned reputation of
being able to talk anyone into anything.

J. P. LEVERITT
Instructor

Handsome J.P. Leveritt, player, coach and trainer

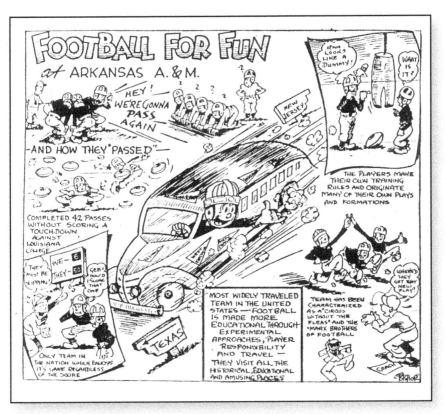

*Newspapers across the country took notice of the
strange football experiment at Arkansas A&M*

The 1940 Wandering Weevils

"Eddie Mac" McMillan of the 1939 Weevils

Members of the 1940 Weevils (from left, top) Pete Cheshire, Ira Jones, Tunis Bishop, Frank "Buddy" Carson, J.P. Leveritt, Van Brewer, Benny Gaston, Terry Field, Norman Wells, Paul Stegall and Verl Gill

The 1941 Wandering Weevils

The Wandering Weevils featured in Collier's magazine, 1940.

WORTH BRUNER
Center

STANLEY CHESHIER
End

GEORGE TILLERY
End

ACROSS THE NATION

Wandering Weevils Worth Bruner, Stanley Cheshire and George Tillery

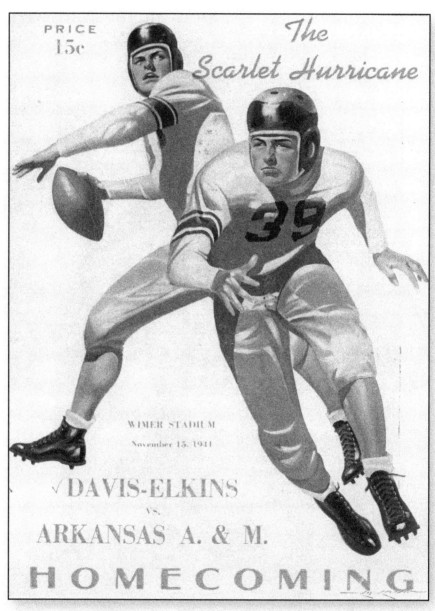

The program cover from the Wandering Weevils game at
Davis & Elkins College in Elkins, West Virginia

The Wandering Weevils were featured in the nationally-syndicated cartoon "Strange As It Seems" by John Hix

| TUNIS BISHOP | COLLIER JORDAN | ROBERT MASKELL | BOYD ARNOLD |
| Fullback | Center | End | Halfback |

Wandering Weevils Tunis Bishop, Collier Jordan,
Robert Maskell and Boyd Arnold

Surviving members of the Wandering Weevils gathered one
more time for a reunion at UAM's 1999 homecoming.

CHAPTER 11

DRUNKS, LEGENDS, AND MOVIE STARS

The trip home from West Virginia was slowed when the bus radiator sprang a leak (Coy Brown suggested they plug it with a chaw of tobacco) and almost came to a screeching halt in Louisville when the boys encountered two well-seasoned ladies of the evening while Ferguson was trying to secure rooms from a balky hotel manager. When Ferguson returned to the bus, the women and some of the players were engaged in financial negotiations. Ferguson ordered the women to take their business down the street, prompting one to ask "What's wrong with the old bastard? Is it all withered up? If he can't, you boys can. He's spoiling your fun." The boys would remind their coach of this exchange for weeks to come.

An irritated Ferguson ordered Beverburg to drive on through the night. The team bus rattled across the cattle guard at the entrance to the Arkansas A&M campus early Monday morning.

The players quickly discovered they were the talk of the school and the town. The prettiest girls on campus wanted to hear stories about the big cities of the East and the boys were all too happy to oblige. The feminine attention and the thought of travel to exotic locations spurred several boys to join the football team until Ferguson ran out of equipment and uniforms.

But not everyone was happy with the football team's growing notoriety. One faculty member confronted Ferguson in the student union and accused him of squandering money while turning the college into a national punch line. President Bankston, seated nearby drinking coffee, jumped to defend his coach. "You're wrong," Bankston said. "Coach will probably make money on every game he plays this fall."

Ferguson called a couple of practices on Tuesday and Wednesday mainly to acquaint the new boys with their teammates. On Thursday, they were off again, this time to the high plains of west Texas to face Daniel Baker College in Odessa. It wasn't much of a contest. Daniel Baker was a veteran, well-drilled team and won easily 33-13, but the fans left the game talking about one of the most bizarre plays they had ever witnessed.

Late in the first half, A&M's Carleton Spears caught a short pass from Annie Robinson, broke into the open field and raced toward the end zone and a certain touchdown. As he neared the goal line, Spears turned and flipped the ball to a startled referee who was following the play. "Why don't you carry it a while," Spears shouted. The confused official dropped the ball and Daniel Baker recovered while the crowd roared in delight.

Spears admitted to Ferguson later that he thought the trailing referee was a teammate. Ferguson just grinned. Tossing the ball to an official would become part of the Boll Weevils' repertoire.

Six days later, on October 20, the Weevils hosted Louisiana College in the first home game of the season. Louisiana College was a Baptist school and Ferguson thought Wildcats coach Jack Walker was a zealot who considered anyone who wasn't a Baptist an infidel. Walker wasn't a fan of Ferguson or his coaching methods and didn't like the idea of playing football for fun. He would teach the Weevils a lesson.

Curious fans and students crowded into Weevils Stadium expecting a comedy show but went away disappointed after the 29-6 A&M loss. Louisiana College played so roughly that the Boll Weevils became angry and forgot all about being funny. The only bright spot was the play of Robinson, who continued to improve as a passer.

The Weevils had two weeks to heal their wounded before their next long trip. They would play the Missouri School of Mines in Rolla, Mo., on November 4 before busing to Cleveland, Ohio for a November 11 date with John Carroll College.

The game in Rolla was the Weevils' fifth since adopting Ferguson's philosophy of playing for laughs. It was certainly the most memorable.

As the team warmed up before a raucous crowd of tough, vocal and inebriated fans, one of the drunkest, with a fifth of whiskey poking out of his coat pocket, wobbled onto the field. Short, stocky and middle-aged, the man spoke with an Eastern European accent so thick he was unintelligible until he began shouting. Rather than push the man away, the Weevils decided to make him their coach for the day and invited him to direct the team as it warmed up. When the rest of the fans realized what was happening, they roared their approval.

Through the first quarter, the Weevils' new "coach" eagerly demonstrated blocking and tackling techniques on the sidelines. Every player he touched or spoke to pretended to pass out from the alcohol fumes.

When the Weevils scored a touchdown, they hoisted their new coach on their shoulders and carried him to the bench like a conquering hero. For the rest of the afternoon, the drunks who had cursed and heckled them before the game became the Weevils' biggest fans. It was a phenomenon that would occur more frequently as the Weevils' reputation spread, with the home teams' fans rooting for the loveable underdogs.

Ferguson watched all these shenanigans with detached bemusement. This was exactly what he had in mind. It was a wild afternoon. Inspired by their new "coach," the Weevils passed from any spot on the field, refused to punt on fourth down and lateraled the ball to teammates for no apparent reason. Every completed pass was followed by a half dozen laterals.

The craziest play began at midfield midway through the first quarter. Robinson retreated to pass only to find himself confronted by an onrushing defender. Rather than be tackled, Robinson flipped the ball backward to a teammate. One lateral followed another as Rolla defenders chased the ball up field. Each time one of the Miners prepared to unload on the ball carrier, he flipped it backward to another Weevil. The last player to handle the ball was guard Coy Brown, who took a lateral in his own end zone and hurled the first pass of his football career, a long throw that was caught and advanced to the Miners' 10-yard line.

Mines coach Gale Bullman had seen enough. He called the officials together and let them know in no uncertain terms that what the Weevils were playing was NOT football. The officials laughed and Bullman stomped off the field and into his own dressing room, not to emerge until the start of the third quarter. When he returned, he was content to laugh along with the fans and gladly accept a 28-13 win. At the end of the game, Bullman offered Ferguson a contract to play again the next year.

The Weevils dressed quickly, got on the bus and headed for their next stop in St. Louis. Ferguson turned them loose for a night on the town and most of the boys made it to bed minutes ahead of the morning sun. Ferguson had stayed out late himself and had just settled in for a few hours sleep when he heard a knock at his hotel room door.

"Coach, I hate to wake you up," whispered the visibly distraught player. "I hope you're feeling good this morning."

"Oh, I guess I'm okay," said a bleary-eyed Ferguson. "What's the matter?"

"Don't think I'm a nut, coach," the boy said, "but I've just had a date with the most wonderful girl on earth and I can't leave St. Louis without seeing her again."

Ferguson studied the desperate young man. "We have to leave this morning," he said. The Weevils were scheduled to spend Sunday night in Chicago.

The boy wouldn't budge. "You want us to have fun on these trips, don't you?" he asked. "Do you want to make me miserable for the rest of my life?"

"No," Ferguson said, "but we have to use some common sense."

"That's not what you've been telling us, and how about what you do yourself?" the boy asked.

Feeling a bit defensive, Ferguson said he had *some* common sense, regardless of overwhelming evidence to the contrary. "Why don't you find the girl, kiss her goodbye and tell her you have to leave." Ferguson suggested.

"I've already kissed her, hugged her, and everything," the boy admitted. "I can't leave without talking things over with her."

Any other college football coach in America would have grabbed the player by his shirt collar and tried to shake some sense into him, or more likely, would have left him in St. Louis. Stewart Ferguson was not any other football coach.

Ferguson decided the team could stay over one more night. He and the players liked St. Louis and who was he to stand in the way of true love. They could travel anytime, he rationalized to himself. Plans were never as important as a city to enjoy or a boy's love.

(A year later, the player married the object of his affection and the couple settled in East St. Louis to raise a family.)

Early Monday morning, Beverburg guided the Arkansas A&M bus across the Mississippi River and into the rich farm land of Illinois. After a stop at Abraham Lincoln's home in Springfield, the bus reached Chicago by dusk. They spent the next two days exploring the city, then headed for South Bend, Indiana and a visit to Notre Dame. Ferguson introduced his players to Elmer Layden, the coach of the Fighting Irish who as a player had been a member of the fabled Four Horsemen. The Weevils watched the Irish practice and soaked in the history and tradition of the university.

The next morning, Ferguson introduced his boys to another coaching legend. Looking for a place to practice, Ferguson had called ahead and secured practice time at the University of Michigan in Ann Arbor. When the Weevils arrived, they were met by Fielding Yost, Michigan's athletic director. Fielding "Hurry Up" Yost was a coaching icon who had guided the Wolverines to six national championships from 1901 to 1926. Ferguson considered Yost to be a coach without peer and was thrilled when he came to the Weevils' practice and spent two hours teaching them some of his favorite plays. Yost took the boys to lunch at the Michigan Union, then wished them well as they boarded their bus for Cleveland.

As Beverburg navigated his way through Detroit, a rotten odor began wafting through the bus. It got so bad Ferguson asked Beverburg to pull over. The smell was coming from Collier Jordan, who had mistaken garlic for onions and consumed an entire bowl during lunch. Terry Field suggested that Jordan hang his head out the window. The players packed the opening around Jordan's head with sweat shirts until the smell became tolerable.

When the Boll Weevils arrived in Cleveland for their game with John Carroll College, the press was waiting, thanks in part to Ferguson's creative advance publicity that generated as many questions as answers. *"When the Arkansas eleven will arrive here, where they'll be coming from and where they'll stay here is all as mysterious as though Garbo herself was in charge,"* reported the *Cleveland Press*. *"Even the team's advance publicity has preserved some mystery. Photographs of a number of Arkansas players have been received at Carroll. But there are no names on the pictures."*

Reporters and photographers from the *Cleveland Plain Dealer* and the *Cleveland News* descended on the team hotel. The next day, the Weevils found themselves splashed across the front pages of both papers. "Arkansas' Famous Boll Weevils Arrive for Game" read the headline in the *Plain Dealer*. "Arkansas Aggies Throw All the Passes But Opponents, Alas, Win All the Games" said the *News*.

Frank Gibbons, a reporter for the *Plain Dealer*, cornered Coy Brown, who was all too happy to talk.

First of all, they want it understood that, although they have lost 15 straight games, they aren't averse to winning. Football is fun for all and all for fun, but they still would like to win.

"Guess we aren't that much different from other humans," grins Coy Brown, captain and guard, who sounds like (Arkansas radio personality) Bob Burns . . . "We play for keeps only the other fella's been doin' the keepin.'

Photos showed Collier Jordan giving a haircut to Carleton Spears; Boyd Arnold and Tunis Bishop clowning with a football, and Robert Maskell, Brown, Spears and Paul Stegall singing in the hotel lobby.

Cleveland News reporter Ed McAuley tried to call Ferguson from the lobby to arrange an interview, but not before he got the runaround from some of the players.

The switchboard girl said Mr. Ferguson didn't answer, but that I could talk to Mr. Brown.

"Yes," said Mr. Brown. "I'm with the Arkansas team, but Mr. Ferguson is not the coach. Mr. Spears is. And you'll probably find out more about it if you call Mr. Bishop."

Your reporter had expected almost anything in his introduction to the Arkansas A and M football team, but this polite doubletalk was distinctly on the bewildering side.

Ferguson finally sauntered across the lobby and introduced himself.

"Oh that," Ferguson laughed when I described the telephone experience. "Never take seriously anything these kids of ours tell you on the phone. Giving folks the run-around is one of their favorite pastimes . . . They're great kids," confided the coach as he walked down Euclid Avenue. "To tell the truth, there are only four or five football players among them, but we have a lot of fun and see a lot of the country . . . And I'll tell you something else. Although we're heavily outweighed and badly outclassed almost every game we play, we haven't had one player injured badly enough to make him miss a single day's practice."

The Boll Weevils were the talk of the town. They ate lunch with Cleveland Mayor Harold Burton and movie star Constance Bennett, who had just completed filming *Topper Takes a Trip* with Cary Grant. The Weevils went coast-to-coast that night when Ferguson and two of his players were interviewed on a nationally-syndicated radio sports program based in Cleveland.

Annie Robinson made sure the folks back home knew what the Weevils were up to, mailing postcards from every stop to *Arkansas*

Gazette Sports Editor Ben Epstein. "For the first time in my life I failed to leave a slick plate at supper," wrote Robinson on one postcard. "There ain't no misery in my stomach even if I did swallow a chicken bone. You see, old pal, I just dined with Constance Bennett and I don't have to tell you any more – do I brother?"

The next day, 3,700 curious spectators braved sleet and an icy wind blowing off Lake Erie to watch this most unusual team from Arkansas. None of the spectators was as curious about the Weevils as John Carroll Coach Tom Conley, who admitted to *Cleveland Press* sports editor Ben Williamson that he scheduled the game without knowing anything about the opponent. Williamson had a field day with the Weevils in his column, headlined "Carroll's Blind Date Makes a Lot of Passes, and Has a Preacher Along — in Case." *"That blind date John Carroll has with Arkansas A and M College at the Stadium Saturday may turn out to be a beaut . . for laughs . . . Coach Tom Conley scheduled the game without knowing anything about the outfit . . . Just answered a letter and said yes."*

Inspired by the publicity, the Boll Weevils put on what the Associated Press called "the wildest football show seen here this season." Cleveland sports writer Howard Preston wrote *"The Marx Brothers of football, the grid team from Arkansas, did everything but saw a woman in half here today . . .* Though the final score was 49-7 (in favor of John Carroll), the Weevils had displayed *"one of the wildest razzle-dazzle attacks ever seen on a Cleveland gridiron."*

When the Boll Weevils returned to Monticello, they were met with a combination of pride, laughter, derision and contempt. Some of the students, faculty and townspeople were thrilled with the national publicity, but many were incensed and thought Ferguson and his team had made the school and the town a national joke.

Newspapers from as far away as Honolulu took note of the goings on while stacks of letters from college presidents, coaches and fans poured in, praising Ferguson and Arkansas A&M for returning the game to the players. One coach even expressed envy for Ferguson's no-win contract.

Many of the local fans thought their coach had lost his mind. "Christ Almighty," complained one, "how can the boys help it when they are coached by a damn, crazy Yankee who should be playing tiddlywinks in the state hospital for nuts."

The Boll Weevils had three games remaining on their schedule – a home game November 17 against Northwest Mississippi Junior College and road games against Hendrix College in Conway, Arkansas November 24 and Missouri State Teachers in Springfield November 30.

As the game with Northwest Mississippi approached, Ferguson found himself being quizzed by fans who wanted to know if his team would play straight football. Would they clown or would they try to win? Just how good was the Mississippi team? Ferguson knew most of the questions came from gamblers who were searching for inside information before placing a wager on the game. Ferguson downplayed his team's chances and after sneaking a peak at the Mississippi aggregation as they entered a local hotel the night before the game, told one curious fan that the Weevils would be lucky to hold them to 40 points. The word got out and bettors started giving the Weevils and 40.

Game day was a postcard perfect autumn afternoon and a capacity crowd, including a large number of alumni returning for homecoming, filled Weevils Stadium. Northwest Mississippi fumbled the opening kickoff on its own two-yard line, the Weevils scored in two plays and Arkansas A&M was on its way to a stunning 26-6 victory, Ferguson's first as head coach after 24 consecutive defeats.

The Weevils scored all 26 points in the first half, then spent the second half at their clowning best. The players cracked the whip as they broke their huddle, skipping, marching like soldiers or winding like a snake. Instead of using numbers for signals, they chanted rhymes:

"Here we come, you sons of guns, you'd better lay 'cause we're making hay."

Most plays in the second half involved multiple laterals and from time to time, the Weevils would tell the Mississippi defenders what play they were going to run.

The A&M victory didn't please many of the locals, who had wagered — and lost — a considerable sum of money on what they thought was a sure thing. There were scattered applause and a few boos as the Weevils left the field, confirming Ferguson's long-standing view of the average football fan.

A 34-14 loss to Hendrix College in Conway preceded the season finale against Missouri State Teachers College in Springfield. The game with Missouri Teachers was a contest Ferguson wanted to win. Ferguson was interested in securing a job at the Missouri school and wanted his team to make a good impression.

It had been raining for 24 hours straight when A&M captain Coy Brown met the Missouri captain in the middle of the field for the coin toss. The Missouri squad was already on the field, huddled in a tight knot on the home sideline. Ferguson had instructed his players to stay in the dressing room to stay dry as long as possible.

Ferguson was already on the opposing sideline when he was startled by a loud chorus of quacking. The Weevils emerged from their dressing room and headed for the field, waddling in a straight line like ducks, flapping their arms and quacking, occasionally flopping face down in pools of water. The few fans who braved the miserable weather were delighted with the show.

As the game commenced, the Weevils continued the silliness, quacking signals, flapping their arms during plays and cleaning their mud-caked hands on the Missouri players' jerseys. And somehow they managed to play good football, at least on defense, allowing just one touchdown in the game's first five minutes in a 7-0 loss.

The '39 Weevils won one game, lost nine, traveled more than 7,000 miles, generated reams of newspaper publicity and goodwill at every stop, and managed to turn a $1,700 profit to boot, the first time in school history the program had finished in the black. The Weevils were America's loveable losers playing a serious game strictly for the fun of it. They were appreciated by fans everywhere, except by those in Monticello.

Incredibly, five members of the team captured postseason honors. Annie Robinson and Stanley Cheshier were named to the All-Arkansas Team for players from small colleges while Coy Brown, Boyd Arnold and Terry Field received honorable mention recognition.

As the season came to an end, Ferguson was receiving heavy criticism from townspeople and even he began to wonder if he had carried a good thing too far. Some of the A&M faculty were upset that the players were gone from campus for long stretches and missing considerable class time. Ferguson made cursory efforts to teach classes on the bus, but for the most part the boys' education came from their travel experiences. None of them seemed to suffer from their absences thanks to Ferguson, who made sure his players posted (but not necessarily earned) a higher combined grade point average than the student body at large.

With no games to coach, Ferguson became a sought-after speaker during the offseason and was elected vice chairman of the Southern Physical Education Association. At the organization's annual meeting in Tulsa, Okla., the local papers praised Ferguson's play-for-fun philosophy as "the most sensational and revolutionary idea advanced at the convention."

Ferguson admitted later that he wasn't trying to change the conduct of football or reform the sport. He was simply trying to keep the sport alive any way he could while staying true to his convictions that the game should be enjoyed by those who played.

CHAPTER 12

Play Football, See the Country

Buddy Carson studied the hand-written note posted on the bulletin board in the Student Union:

Any boy who wants to travel from New York to California should join the football team. See Coach Ferguson at the practice field.

Carson hadn't planned to play football in college but was intrigued by the opportunity to see the country. He had played at Monticello High School despite struggling to keep 150 pounds on his 5-8 frame. He had seen action at quarterback and halfback and was an accurate passer up to 30 yards but what he did best was punt. Monticello High played its home games at the college stadium and Carson once launched a quick-kick 86 yards thanks to a 40 mile per hour wind at his back and a generous roll. (The punt is still a stadium record.)

Carson had never met Ferguson but followed the Weevils

closely in the newspapers. When he showed up at practice that afternoon, he sized up his new coach and was unimpressed. He didn't look like a coach, Carson thought. Nor did he sound like one. Ferguson never raised his voice, never cursed. In fact, he didn't say much at all, at least not in practice.

J. P. Leveritt thought Ferguson almost timid, his voice often trailing off to a whisper. But occasionally, the coach would surprise his players, as he did the day he lined up three defenders in practice to show his ball carriers how to avoid tackles. Unaware their coach had been a standout player in college, they were stunned as he feinted one way, then another, and avoided all three defenders.

To his players, Ferguson was a bundle of contradictions. He married his secretary, Edna McAdam, 20 years his junior, on June 6, 1940, ending what had been a scandal in Monticello. The marriage also put a serious crimp in his womanizing, at least as long as he stayed in town. When Ferguson was at home, he was the picture of a devoted husband. On the road was another story. Ferguson had earned the nickname "Gee Gosh" from his players, a phrase he used repeatedly at the sight of an attractive female. With gaunt features and a slight build, he hardly looked the part of a lady's man, but most of the players knew their coach had a line of bullshit that was surprisingly effective with the opposite sex. Many of the older players knew about Ferguson's womanizing, but never said much, even when Ferguson would disappear from time to time in the company of a young woman, leaving the boys to sightsee on their own.

Ferguson would have plenty of opportunities for female attention in 1940. The schedule called for the Weevils to travel more than 10,000 miles through 27 states with games scheduled within a mile of both the Atlantic and Pacific Oceans. As he had in 1939, Ferguson scheduled just two home games and only one game with an Arkansas opponent.

THE 1940 SCHEDULE

Sept.	16	Louisiana College	Pineville, Louisiana
Sept.	28	Eastern Kentucky Teachers	Richmond, Kentucky
Oct.	4	Lebanon Valley	Hershey, Pennsylvania
Oct.	11	North Texas State	Denton, Texas
Oct.	19	University of Nevada	Reno, Nevada
Oct.	23	Humboldt State	Eureka, California
Oct.	28	South Dakota Mines	Rapid City, South Dakota
Nov.	1	Hendrix	Monticello, Arkansas
Nov.	16	Hofstra College	Hempstead, New York
Nov.	21	Missouri State Teachers	Springfield, Missouri
No.	27	NW Mississippi JC	Monticello, Arkansas

Ferguson had little trouble finding opponents, receiving offers from nearly 50 schools who saw the Boll Weevils and their comedy act as box office gold. While most of the Weevils' slapstick was spontaneous and within the context of the games, the comedy was evolving, with players dreaming up skits and rehearsing them before springing them on unsuspecting opponents. A favorite ploy was the "Whirlwind," with players milling around the ballcarrier in ever-widening circles until everyone got dizzy and sat down. The increasing reliance on comedy was due in part to the players buying in to Ferguson's plan and in part to necessity. The Weevils were sorely lacking in football talent.

Only eight players returned from the '39 team with most of the best players either out of eligibility or in the military. The Weevils had a strong local flavor with six boys from Monticello – Carson, Stanley and Pete Cheshier, twin brothers Ralph and Paul Stegall, and Verl Gill. The other returnees were Tunis Bishop, Worth Bruner, Terry Field, J. P. Leveritt and Robert Maskell. One important player was missing.

Annie Robinson was married and his new wife didn't think

playing football was a proper way to earn a living. She also objected to the idea of her young husband being gone for weeks at a time traveling the country and no doubt enjoying the company of assorted females. Pete Cheshier would have to replace Robinson.

As the Weevils prepared for their season opener at Louisiana College, newspapers across the country were paying notice. Large stories in the *Birmingham Post, Tulsa Daily World* and the *New York Herald Tribune* informed their readers of the strange football experiment taking place at Arkansas A&M. Ferguson enjoyed the attention immensely, regaling reporters with his unorthodox notions. No, he didn't teach his players to block, he said, explaining that the best way to block was to "step on the other guy's toes." As for tackling, Ferguson didn't teach that either and the Weevils never tackled in practice. "A boy doesn't need to be taught to tackle," he said. "That comes naturally. Practice just makes them tackle-shy. Besides, it would spoil our jersey-tackling and arm grabbing, which are something extraordinary." The Weevils passed the ball on almost every play, said Ferguson, because a running game required blockers and "blockers are likely to get wounded. On our offense, the interference follows the ball carrier. When the ball carrier sees he can't go forward he laterals the ball to the next man. You haven't any blockers that way but you have more ball carriers."

Ferguson made sure his players not only played funny, but looked funny. In addition to the garish yellow and green uniforms of the previous season, he had collected boxes of salesmen's samples in all colors and sizes. He left it up to the players to choose which jerseys they wanted to wear, and if they wanted to change to a different color at halftime, that was okay too.

When the Weevils boarded their bus for Pineville, Louisiana on September 16, the words "Wandering Boll Weevils" were emblazoned on both the front and back. Expecting players to be enticed by the prospect of coast-to-coast travel, Ferguson had ordered

30 complete uniforms, but he needed only 23 for the first game. In fact, the Weevil roster changed as the season progressed with players coming and going. Ferguson would occasionally ask J. P. Leveritt to grab two or three boys from a physical education or tumbling class and bring them along to fill out the squad.

The Weevils were no match for Louisiana College, losing 28-0. Cheshier struggled to duplicate Robinson's magic in the air but the new players managed to catch on to the clowning style. A few of them with no football experience made their first tackle in a football game.

All the boys had played well enough to leave Ferguson in a quandary. He could only take 22 on the long trip to Pennsylvania and would be forced to leave one player at home. His problem was solved on the bus ride back from Pineville. At a rest stop in a small Louisiana town, one of the players fell asleep on the toilet and Ferguson left after failing to count heads to see if all the players were back on the bus. The drowsy Weevil had won the lottery and would be forced to stay in Monticello.

Ferguson spent the next few days preparing for the long road trip to the east coast, still wondering if his Weevils could avoid total embarrassment without Robinson. Near midnight on the day before the team was scheduled to leave, Ferguson was dozing in his office when Robinson appeared in his doorway. The chance to see the country was too much for Annie, who had managed to sneak out and leave behind an angry wife and mother-in-law.

"Can I still have a uniform, coach?" Robinson asked. He could have any one he wanted said a beaming Ferguson. But there was work to do. The team would leave in a matter of hours and Robinson was not enrolled. Ferguson rang door bells and rattled screen doors to wake up the faculty members he needed to get Robinson enrolled for the fall semester. A few hours later, the bus – with Robinson safely aboard – left for Richmond, Kentucky and a game with Eastern Kentucky Teachers College.

Eastern Kentucky had a new, hard-nosed coach, Rome Rankin, and a newfound commitment to winning football. To Rankin, football was a serious endeavor and Arkansas A&M's clowning was an affront to his football sensibilities. Eastern Kentucky spent much of the game trying to deal out as much punishment as possible en route to a 39-0 victory. It got so rough that Ferguson decided it wasn't safe for him to stand too close to the sideline.

The Weevils did manage some daffiness in spite of Eastern's best efforts. Late in the first half the Weevils found themselves on the Maroon's one yard line, first and goal. A&M lined up to run Ferguson's favorite play, the Swinging Gate. At the snap of the ball a free-for-all began as Robinson, Tunis Bishop and Stanley Cheshier took turns tossing the ball backward to each other as the action moved away from the Eastern goal line. Up the field they went with the Eastern defense in pursuit. As the ball neared the A&M goal line, Robinson heaved a long pass downfield. The errant throw was intercepted by a Kentucky defender and returned for a touchdown.

At the half, a disappointed Ferguson approached Robinson in the dressing room. Why had he called that kind of play, Ferguson wanted to know. Grinning mischievously, Robinson said, "Coach, I just had to fool you that time."

The Weevils made it out of Kentucky in one piece and headed for Pennsylvania and an October 4 date with Lebanon Valley College in Hershey, Pennsylvania, the home of Hershey chocolate.

Ferguson had devoted considerable time promoting the game in Hershey hoping to attract a large gate that would be split evenly between A&M, Lebanon Valley and the Hershey estate. He had even managed to talk freelance writer Kyle Crichton to drive down from New York to write a feature story on his team for *Collier's* magazine. While Ferguson focused on A&M's reputation for football follies, his counterpart at Lebanon Valley, an overzealous and very serious press agent, was billing the game as the second installment of the Battle of Gettysburg.

In deference to their nickname, the Weevils took a circuitous route to Hershey, wandering through the pastoral hills of Maryland, driving through a small corner of Delaware just to say they had been there, then circling back through the small towns of southeastern Pennsylvania.

Ferguson had booked rooms at the Hershey Inn, a picturesque and neatly kept little hotel on East Chocolate Avenue less than a mile from the Hershey factory. Shortly after settling in, Ferguson received a call from Crichton in New York. He was sending world-reknowned photographer Hans Von Groenhoff to take photos of the team to accompany his feature story. Hans Herman Hugo Ernest Wilhelm Von Groenhoff's photos had appeared in most of the major magazines of the day, including *Life, Newsweek,* and *Time.*

Ferguson was thrilled by the news, then began to worry that his team wouldn't present Von Groenhoff with anything worth shooting, but the famous photographer put everyone at ease and proved to be a delight – to both Ferguson and the players. The stay in Hershey was one of the team's most enjoyable. They toured the Hershey Chocolate factory, devouring all the chocolate they could eat, and were treated like visiting royalty.

When it finally came time to play the football game, the Weevils marveled at Lebanon Valley's beautiful stadium and pristinely manicured field. As Buddy Carson and some of his teammates warmed up under the stadium lights, they sat down on the lush turf, then laid on the ground and looked up at the stars. God amighty, thought Carson, this is a good field.

The Weevils wouldn't get to play on it long. Before the game, Lebanon Valley officials approached Ferguson and informed him there would be no timeouts, no pauses in the action, and very little break at halftime. Hershey was a factory town and the game had to be over by 9 p.m. so the fans could be at work for the start of the 10 o'clock shift.

Lebanon Valley scored three touchdowns in the first quarter and won easily, 28-6. The only highlight for the Weevils came late in the contest when Orien Gates, one of A&M's slowest players, intercepted a lateral and lumbered 60 yards for a touchdown. Von Groenhoff captured the moment on the Weevils' sideline, snapping a photo of an excited Ferguson and his players as they cheered for their teammate.

When the Weevils reluctantly left Hershey, they had an extra passenger on the bus. Von Groenhoff rode with the team as far as Washington, photographing the players during a stop at the Gettysburg battlefield.

The long trek back to Arkansas took the team through the Blue Ridge Mountains of Virginia. The mountains were ablaze in fall color and Ferguson directed Beverhurg to turn off the main highway for a closer look. The Weevils stopped long enough in one mountain hamlet to enjoy a huge meal of ham, fried potatoes, sweet corn and thick slabs of apple pie. Anxious to make time, Ferguson ordered his team back on the road and they drove into the night, headed for Roanoke. Everyone was asleep but Beverburg, and when the bus driver began scratching his head and talking loudly to himself to stay awake, Ferguson knew it was time to stop.

He located a hotel in Roanoke for what seemed like a bargain, but as he climbed the musty stairs to his third floor room, Ferguson realized where he was. He had booked his team in a whorehouse!

As he reached the second floor, he found his players surrounded by a large group of girls. One of the younger boys, who obviously had no experience in such matters, grabbed Ferguson's sleeve. "Coach, these are the friendliest girls I've ever met," said the awestruck boy. "Must be the Virginia hospitality we've heard so much about."

Ferguson quickly rounded up his players and explained that the girls wanted business, not dates. He then loudly asked if any of the boys had any spending money. He knew they were all broke and when they confirmed his suspicions, the girls grew decidedly less friendly. One of the girls suggested that Ferguson loan the boys some money and his fun would be on the house. Ferguson may have enjoyed female company, but he had his standards and he wasn't about to finance a night of sex for his players.

After ordering the boys to their rooms, he settled in for an uneasy night's sleep that was interrupted by a knock at the door. One of the older boys needed to borrow two dollars. Ferguson told him it would take a lot more than that to cure him after a night with one of the girls, then sent him back to his room. Ferguson spent the remainder of the night pacing the halls to make sure no one else gave in to temptation.

The bus rolled onto the Arkansas A&M campus late on the night of October 7. Two days later, the Weevils would begin the longest trip of their lives, a month-long jaunt that would take them across the continental divide, up the west coast and back through the Rocky Mountains.

Stewart Ferguson had much work to do, including convincing his boys they could play without their leader.

CHAPTER 13

THE WILD WEST

When the Boll Weevils returned from Pennsylvania, Annie Robinson left the team for good. He had received several telegrams from his new bride threatening divorce if he didn't come home. Ferguson didn't have time to worry about finding Robinson's replacement; he had much to do. The bus needed repairs and he had to handle the logistics of feeding and lodging 22 boys for 31 days.

The first stop on the western tour was Denton, Texas for a game with North Texas State. As usual, the trip was anything but smooth. Before reaching the Texas state line, Ferguson had to warn Beverburg to quit stopping the bus every few miles and threatening to fight Carson and the Stegall boys, who were battling their own boredom by picking at the high-strung bus driver.

Another problem arose when an inordinately shy freshman was unable to urinate in front of the other players. Ferguson had ordered Beverburg to quit stopping at one-hole gas stations to relieve the players. It took too long. Just pull over on the side of the road and they could all go at once. The strategy worked for everyone but the boy with the reluctant bladder.

Ferguson and the other players tried to loosen up their embarrassed teammate with jokes and Beverburg even drained warm water from the radiator to pour on his hand. Nothing worked.

Later that afternoon near the Arkansas-Texas state line, the boy stood by a bush for 15 minutes, unable to relieve himself. Finally, the other players came up with a solution. As the bus rolled into Texas, the boy was stripped of his pants and underwear and forced to sit in his seat naked from the waist down for the next two hours. As his teammates made comments about his manhood, the half-dressed lad began to lose his shyness. At the next stop, he was first off the bus and the first to take care of business.

The game with North Texas was both a one-sided blowout and a rip-roaring success, at least from Ferguson's point of view. North Texas scored at will, hammering the Weevils 79-0. As the Eagles' swift backs raced through the A&M defense, Weevil players formed an 11-man funnel and directed them toward the goal line. Once in a while, mostly as a surprise, a Weevil made a half-hearted effort at tackling someone.

On offense, the Weevils turned and punted the ball toward their own goal line. When the head linesman penalized A&M for being offside, one of the players took the official's penalty flag and tied it around his head like a blindfold. On one play, the boys concealed the game ball and used a six-inch toy football, tossing it to a startled North Texas defender, who, thinking he had an interception, raced down field for a touchdown. Naturally, A&M was penalized on the play. In fact, the Weevils had three touchdowns nullified by what the officials deemed illegal tomfoolery.

After the game, two North Texas professors were waiting for Ferguson outside the visitors' dressing room. It was the first game they had ever really enjoyed, they said. Later, at the team hotel, three of the best players on the North Texas team approached Ferguson. They wanted to play for Arkansas A&M. Could they join the team right now? Ferguson considered the three for a moment, but fortunately, the bus was full, preventing a serious breech of his own ethics.

The North Texas game was played on Friday and by early Saturday morning, the Wandering Weevils were headed west to spend the night in Tucumcari, New Mexico. They had eight days before their next game on October 19 against the University of Nevada in Reno and they would spend most of the time sightseeing. The next day included a stop in Albuquerque and a drive through the Painted Desert at sunset before their next overnight stay in Holbrook, Arizona. By the time they reached Flagstaff, the bus needed repairs to its brakes, so the boys loosened up with a light workout at Northern Arizona College.

When the bus was repaired, Ferguson suggested a side trip to the Grand Canyon but the boys had Hollywood on their minds – or more accurately Hollywood starlets. They went to the Grand Canyon anyway and the boys were amazed by one of the world's great natural wonders. "Coach, we would have left you home on the next trip if you'd let us miss this sight," said one grateful player.

Before they left, the boys loaded up on souvenirs at a park gift shop. Unfortunately, they neglected to pay for any of them. In all their travels, Ferguson had rarely had to worry about his players taking things from hotels or restaurants and on the whole was proud of his team's behavior.

Not this time.

As they started to leave, park police stopped the bus. Ferguson got off, and after a lengthy discussion with the officers, stepped back on carrying a bushel basket. "Now if everybody will put the stuff that they pilfered into this basket," said Ferguson, "they said they would let us go." By the time Ferguson reached the back of the bus, the basket was full.

They reached Boulder Dam (later Hoover Dam) just after

midnight. Ignoring the late hour, the boys clambered out of the bus to get a better look at the huge edifice bathed in floodlights. When they got back on the bus, they were asleep in minutes, but Las Vegas was still wide awake by the time they reached the Strip. Ferguson located rooms at bargain prices at the Overland Hotel, then turned the boys loose, knowing their empty pockets would keep them out of serious trouble.

Most of the boys were initially reluctant to walk into the casinos and since none of them had any money, the gaming houses quickly lost their appeal. The boys managed three to four hours of sleep before they were back on the bus and headed to California.

Los Angeles was everything the players had hoped it would be and more. They spent the next two days on a non-stop tour of the city, visiting Warner Brothers Studios, the LaBrea Tar Pits, and the L.A. Coliseum, where they worked out under the tutelage of Howard "Biff" Jones, the legendary coach of the University of Southern California. Jones had won his fourth national championship at USC the previous season and the players were star-struck as he taught them one of the Trojans' pet plays.

The Weevils had a tour guide during their stay in Los Angeles. Sidney Johnson, the business manager of the *Los Angeles Times*, had a relative on the Arkansas A&M faculty and agreed to show Ferguson and his team around the city.

Knowing the players would like to meet some girls, Johnson rounded up a bevy of beautiful UCLA coeds to show the boys a good time on their first night in town. Some of the boys were so intimidated by the glamorous ladies that it was decided they would all go out together in one big group.

While the boys were on their own, Johnson took Ferguson to dinner at a swanky Hollywood restaurant. As they waited for a table behind a velvet rope, Ferguson struck up a conversation with a stunning blonde. When she was escorted to her table, Ferguson turned to Johnson. "You know, she looks just like Betty Grable," Ferguson said, referring to the actress whose iconic bathing suit photo would make her the number one pin-up girl of GI's during World War II.

"That was Betty Grable," said Johnson as Ferguson's knees buckled.

****

Before leaving Monticello, Ferguson had contacted Arkansas-born radio star Bob Burns and Burns graciously invited Ferguson and his team to visit his 600-acre ranch when they reached Los Angeles.

In 1940, Bob Burns was one of America's biggest radio stars. Born in Greenwood, Arkansas and raised in Van Buren, Burns had become famous as a self-effacing rustic bumpkin with humorous stories about his "kinfolks" back home in "Arkinsaw." Part of his act included playing a homemade musical instrument he had constructed out of a piece of pipe. Burns called it a bazooka and soon, Arkansas was being referred to as bazooka land in the national press. (The army later borrowed the name for its World War II anti-tank weapon.) To listeners across the country, Burns was the only thing they knew about Arkansas and his act reinforced negative stereotypes.

But Burns never forgot his roots, and welcomed the Weevils with open arms. The boys were wide-eyed, having never seen a home quite so large, especially one with a three-car garage. Burns bounded into the living room in shirt sleeves, introduced his wife, and immediately put Ferguson and the boys at ease. Burns may have been a big star, Buddy Carson thought, but he's one of us.

Burns was a regular on the Kraft Music Hall radio program hosted by Bing Crosby and invited the whole team to the show that night. Crosby was vacationing in Spain so Burns was the guest host and called Ferguson and a couple of players on stage for a little light-hearted banter during the broadcast. The boys were entranced with Dorothy Lamour, who appeared that night as Burns' guest. The players learned that in radio, the stars read from their script, then dropped the pages on the floor so they wouldn't get confused and repeat their lines. Several of the players snatched up the pages and took them as souvenirs.

Everywhere the Weevils went in Los Angeles, they cut a wide swath. The bus itself was an attention getter as Beverburg weaved erratically down Hollywood Boulevard. "Wandering Boll Weevils" was emblazoned in gold on the front and back, and the team's schedule was printed in bold letters on both sides. The boys were dressed in white coveralls with Arkansas A&M printed in bold green letters across the backs. Ferguson never missed an opportunity to promote his team or the college.

Before they left town, *Los Angeles Times* sports editor Paul Zimmerman let his readers know about the strange football team from Arkansas that had been roaming the streets of their city.

Visitor in this village yesterday was one of the "travelingest" football teams in the country representing Arkansas A&M, and the story back of it would put the imagination of a movie script writer to shame . . . This bus load of gridsters that paused here for "educational sight-seeing" is en route to Reno for a game with the University of Nevada this weekend. It has already been as far east as Hershey, Pa., and before the snow flies will be hitting the pike for home after a trip to New York City . . . They are in the game for the fun of it. The players can and do improvise new stuff in the huddle. There is no "how come" accounting to the coach afterward. Coach Ferguson urges the boys to be original.

Zimmerman closed his column with an appeal to the organizers of the Rice Bowl, a Christmas-day game to be played in the Rose Bowl to provide relief help for China, to invite the Boll Weevils back to play in the game.

Before the Weevils left Los Angeles, they enjoyed one more night on the town, dining at Eaton's Rancho, a Hollywood restaurant and watering hole for the rich and famous. When the team arrived, Roy Rogers was standing outside the restaurant and Jeanette McDonald was in the main dining room. The boys were still wide-eyed when they piled on the bus and headed for Nevada.

CHAPTER 14

Marion Motley

Monticello, Arkansas was very much part of the Jim Crow South in 1940. The players on the Arkansas A&M football team had grown up in a culture of segregated hotels, restaurants, and most certainly, public schools.

Arkansas A&M was itself an all-white institution and would remain so for the next 27 years. Race mixing was not tolerated in polite society and blacks and whites had little contact, none on the playing fields of athletic competition.

For the Wandering Weevils, that was about to change.

The University of Nevada had a huge black halfback named Marion Motley who weighed close to 30 pounds more than the biggest player on the A&M roster. He was also fast.

Most of the Wandering Weevils had grown up accepting institutionalized racism as a way of life. It was all they knew and no one questioned what was considered the natural order of things. The players, or at least most of them, clung to the same prejudices and preconceived notions about blacks – or "coloreds" as they were referred to by more enlightened whites.

None of the boys had ever played against blacks in football or any other athletic competition. Most believed what they had been told – if you hit a nigger hard a couple of times, he'll quit.

Buddy Carson knew better. Frank Carson, Sr., owned a grocery store in Monticello which sold to both whites and blacks. For as long as Buddy could remember, a black man named Jude Bains had lived in a makeshift apartment in a barn on the Carsons' farm. "Jude didn't have much education," remembered Carson, "but he was smart. He worked two or three jobs and saved his money. Jude hunted foxes and coons with Daddy all his life. He was sort of like family. I guess that's why I never had the typical southern attitude towards 'em. Jude worked hard all the time. He lived to be 100 years old, and when he died, he had saved $100,000."

Carson knew his teammates were wrong about blacks being afraid of physical contact. What they were afraid of was making life difficult for their parents if they hit the wrong white boy. "I found out in high school, from talking to some colored boys, that they'd been told by their mommas and daddys – 'Don't you get in a fight with Mr. Frank's boy. Don't beat him up. He'll cut my credit off.' Daddy wouldn't have done it, but they thought he would."

The Weevils arrived in Reno barely 12 hours before their scheduled kickoff with Nevada. It had been an adventure coaxing the bus and its boiling radiator over the Sierra Nevada Mountains.

It was an expected courtesy of the times for northern schools to ask southern teams whether they minded playing against blacks and to inform them if they had black players on their team. No one from Nevada had mentioned it to Ferguson, who found out about Motley when the team reached its hotel.

Ferguson knew it would be a challenge to convince the majority of his team to play against a negro. Ferguson was no champion of racial equality, but this was a chance for his boys to learn an important lesson about people and broaden their view of the world, something he had hoped for when he scheduled games all over the country.

The players didn't have much time to protest. They were exhausted from travel and lack of sleep and had barely practiced in the last two weeks. The game was ugly from the start. Motley and company ran roughshod over the outclassed Weevils, winning 78-0. Motley scored five touchdowns, mostly on long runs, and may have changed a few attitudes in the Weevil huddle. After one thunderous run in which he flattened half the defense, the stunned players wobbled back to the huddle. "I don't believe he's gonna quit, no matter how many times we hit him," said one player. "I'd like to have a couple of boys like that on our team."

Years later, the players would gain an even greater appreciation for Motley, who went on to earn All-America honors at the University of Oregon before playing eight seasons with the Cleveland Browns and being elected to the Pro Football Hall of Fame.

Facing Motley may not have turned the boys into abolitionists, but it gave them something to think about.

The Weevils spent two more days in Reno, enjoying the food and hospitality of a city that most would remember as one of their favorite stops. Reno was a wide-open city with gambling and legal prostitution. Ferguson warned his players to stay away from the Stockade, the city's most famous brothel, then with the boys out from under foot, headed straight for it. The coach wandered aimlessly around the circular boardwalk of rooms, sizing up the various offerings of sin which came in all shapes, sizes and prices. As he began his second trip around with serious thought to making a purchase, a voice from one of the rooms called out "Here comes that cheap guy again." The next thing Ferguson heard was a snicker. He turned and there stood half his football team. Some of the boys had been trying to talk the girls into a free ride when they spotted their coach. Ferguson was mortified and left, but a few of the more persuasive boys managed to get what they came for.

CHAPTER 15

FERGIE COMES HOME

Thanks to some bad advice from a well-meaning truck driver, the Weevils spent a harrowing night navigating a treacherous road over the Sierra Nevadas on their way to Eureka, California, a small community on the Pacific coast 270 miles north of San Francisco. They were scheduled to play Humboldt State on October 23 in nearby Arcata.

Before leaving Reno, Beverburg stopped for gas and met a trucker who told him about a short-cut through the mountains that would cut 35 miles off their trip. He failed to mention that the short-cut was a winding, steep, dangerously narrow gravel road strewn with larger rocks. Ferguson and his players saw their lives flash before their eyes as Beverburg maneuvered his way over the mountains, rarely taking the bus out of second gear. A pale moon illuminated the cliffs on one side of the road; on the other side was a seemingly bottomless black chasm. Three times Ferguson instructed Beverburg to stop the bus, fearful that the road was too dangerous, but each time decided it was riskier to stay in one place and count on the brakes to keep them from rolling down the steep grades.

When they reached Eureka and the Pacific coast, it started to rain and didn't stop for the next two days. By game day it was still pouring and the field was a quagmire. Ferguson told the last 11 players to get dressed that they would have to start while he and the remaining players climbed into the stands and covered up in rain slickers to stay dry until halftime.

The Weevils on the field had their fun, paddling interference for ball carriers, making sounds like river steamboats when snapping the ball, and yelling "ship ahoy" at Humboldt ball carriers. The boys on the field took off their shoes and socks and halfback Bennie Gaston stripped to his jock strap, after which the Humboldt defenders seemed reluctant to make a tackle. A&M lost 13-0, Ferguson collected their pay check, and the boys were on their way again.

Next stop – Rapid City and a game with the South Dakota School of Mines after a detour through the Redwood forest. The boys were stunned by the giant trees and gave Beverburg a hard time when he managed to get the bus stuck while trying to drive through a tunnel carved in one of them. Their good humor was gone by the time they reached South Dakota; they were tired, irritable and sick of each other's company. Ferguson had ordered Beverburg to stop the bus in the middle of the Wyoming prairie for a light practice, hoping to work off some of the boys' pent-up anger and boredom. The trip across Nevada had offered little in the way of sightseeing, the boys were unimpressed with what they viewed as unfriendly Salt Lake City, and the prairies of Wyoming seemed to stretch on forever. By the time they reached Rapid City, they were in no mood to be the football clowns they were advertised to be in the local paper.

Ferguson wanted to beat South Dakota but couldn't bring himself to encourage his boys' best effort, since he'd done nothing to prepare them for real football success. Many of his former players from Dakota Wesleyan were now high school football coaches in the state and would be at the game. Ferguson wanted to show them that their old coach still knew a thing or two about the sport.

The South Dakota papers took note of Ferguson's return. A banner headline in the *Sioux Falls Argus Leader* proclaimed:

Little Fergy (Remember Him?) Preaches Fun Football
Just Tells His Boys Rules, Turns 'Em Loose in Ten States

Look out South Dakota, Stewart A. Ferguson is coming back and what a comeback that homecoming will be. The former coach of the Dakota Wesleyan Tigers now travels with the screwiest, most unorthodox football aggregation in the land, the Arkansas A. and M. Boll Weevils. The Weevils will play the School of Mines at Rapid City (Monday) night. And to top it off, Fergie probably is the most envied man in the grid coaching fraternity.

He doesn't worry, hunt for material (sic), care much whether he wins his games, sometimes doesn't show up for practice, turns all responsibility of making up plays and formations to his players while he sits back and enjoys the steady employment benefits of a full professorship.

Ferguson didn't have to tell his players that this was a game he wanted to win. He was wound tighter than usual, the boys thought. Ferguson had never gotten over the hurt of being fired by Dakota Wesleyan and was afraid a poor performance would wipe out what was left of his coaching legacy in the state.

As the Weevils put on their uniforms before the game, Ferguson could see they were travel weary. He desperately wanted to give them a rousing pep talk but thought it would have little effect.

He turned the lights off in the dressing room and urged them to rest and suggested that if they were going to try anything flashy or different, they should do it early while they still had the energy to pull it off.

South Dakota Coach Art Sullivan had promised to play straight football and said the only concession he would make to the Weevils' style of play was to loosen up his defense to protect against A&M's passing. Apparently, his team didn't listen.

On the Weevils' first play from scrimmage, quarterback Pete Cheshier called for a deep pass. At the snap, J. P. Leveritt streaked up the right sideline past three South Dakota defenders. Cheshier's high, arcing toss was underthrown and looked like a certain interception. Leveritt reversed his field and came back for the ball, leaping high in front of the South Dakota defenders to make the catch, then whirled away from one defender, broke an attempted tackle and set sail for the end zone. He shook off another would-be tackler at the South Dakota 20. As he neared the end zone he shocked players, officials and fans by turning hand springs over the goal line. Ferguson later called it the greatest single play he had ever seen in football. The crowd sat in stunned silence for a moment, then burst into cheers. They were still cheering when Ferguson took Leveritt by the arm, guided him behind the bench to a spot in front of the grandstands, and instructed Leveritt to show the South Dakota fans why he was considered one of the top gymnasts in the South. Leveritt entertained the crowd with a series of flips and acrobatics.

The Weevils were on a roll and Ferguson was coaching, not just watching. Moments later, they caught South Dakota off guard with the "sleeper play." Leveritt motioned a teammate to come to the sideline, then slipped on to the edge of the field in front of the A&M bench, unnoticed and uncovered. His 31-yard reception set up another touchdown and the Weevils had a shocking 13-0 lead.

By halftime it was 26-0 and the players carried Ferguson to the dressing room on their shoulders. "You're too tired to watch us do anything except lick 'em tonight," said one player.

It was the best half of football by an A&M team in a decade and confirmed Ferguson's suspicions that had this bunch played it straight, they might have been a competitive football team – not as much fun, but competitive. Pete Cheshier was brilliant, zipping passes to his brother Stanley as well as Leveritt and Benny Gaston. Pete Cheshier completed 12 of 19 throws in the first half for 203 yards and three touchdowns and scored one on a short run.

"I'm still wondering who taught him to pass," Ferguson said later. "I didn't."

Ferguson told his players not to score anymore in the second half. Vindication was one thing, but he didn't want anyone to accuse him of using the School of Mines as a scapegoat for what happened at Dakota Wesleyan.

The *Rapid City Daily Journal* was effusive in praise for the Boll Weevils following their unexpected 26-7 victory:

Maybe the Arkansas A. and M. grid aggregation plays for fun and doesn't give a hoot if it wins, but you can't convince the School of Mines Hardrockers that the Aggies from bazooka land are giving anything away.

Last night, the Hardrockers became the first victim in seven starts for the traveling Arkansas gridders, who staged an aerial barrage that had the Miners – and the fans – dizzy from trying to keep track of the flying pigskin . . . the lads from the South earned the respect of the Hardrockers, the fans, and the officials for their clever ball-handling, their sportsmanship, and their fire.

Ferguson was on cloud nine. His team had played brilliantly and he could go back to Arkansas knowing he had burnished his coaching reputation in front of the home folks. The trip home would be a little sweeter.

CHAPTER 16

To Long Island the Hard Way

Three days after the victory in South Dakota, the Weevils rolled into Monticello with 10 hours to spare. That's how much time they had to prepare for their first home game of the season against Hendrix College on November 1.

The players were still bleary-eyed from travel when they trotted onto the field to warm up but managed to play well in a 7-0 loss. The spirited effort even pleased some of the home fans.

The next road trip would begin in a week and Ferguson encouraged his players to go to class and rest as much as possible. This time they would head east, and Ferguson had made allowances for plenty of sightseeing and leisure time without the constant pressure of adhering to a strict schedule.

They left Sunday morning, November 9, with a new driver, Joe Coker, at the wheel of the bus and a full week before their next game against Hofstra University on Long Island, New York. In the meantime, they would make a lazy journey across the heart of Dixie, traveling through Mississippi, Alabama, Georgia and

South Carolina before heading up the Atlantic coast to New York. Ferguson made sure they saw the University of Alabama and there were stops in Atlanta and Athens, where the boys practiced at the University of Georgia.

A tour of Charleston and the South Carolina beaches left the aisle of the bus ankle deep in sea shells and several dead jelly fish. The smell made the boys ride with their heads out the windows until they decided to dispose of at least some of their more odorous cargo.

As they made their way through North Carolina, intermittent rain and thick patches of fog made visibility difficult. As dusk approached, Ferguson cautioned Coker to slow down, then stretched out on the front seat for a nap. While Ferguson slept, the players discussed whether or not to ask each teammate to donate a quarter for a pot to be used to buy a prostitute in the next town of any size. They would draw straws and the winner would receive an hour or two of physical gratification for his 25 cent investment.

Ferguson's nap and the boys' plans were interrupted by the sound of screeching brakes and metal against metal, followed by a bump that nearly turned the bus on its side before it rocked back on all four wheels. Gathering himself, Ferguson made sure all the boys got out through the partially jammed door. Somehow, on a bus with no seat belts, no one was injured, with the exception of Coker, who received a cut over his eye and needed stitches.

Loy Perry broke the tension. As Ferguson and the players stood beside the road in ankle-deep water, Perry stared at the beat-up remains, shook his head and said, "Poor bus." Coach and players broke up in laughter and Ferguson mumbled a quick prayer of thanks.

Coker had plowed into a stalled pick-up truck loaded with wood scraps. The bus was severely damaged and unusable. Moreover, when Ferguson called the A&M business office to alert them to the accident, he discovered the bus was uninsured. The nearest town was Plymouth, North Carolina, which had no hotels, but thanks to the state police and some friendly locals, the boys were shuttled into town and Ferguson found places for them to spend the night in private homes.

From there to New York, a once leisurely trip became an ordeal. Without the funds to pay for a charter, Ferguson and his team crowded onto an All-American Lines bus to Washington, then changed to another bus with a driver who was adamant about not driving a football team anywhere. When the players refused to leave, the driver cursed them, threatened to call the police and hinted at bodily harm. The players, under orders from Ferguson, who was cowering at the back of the bus, just grinned at the antagonistic driver. The other passengers were won over by the smiling players and the driver finally relented.

The Weevils stopped in Philadelphia for a one-night stay that included a tour of Independence Hall and a close-up look at the Liberty Bell. That night, Tunis Bishop came to the hotel with two gallons of peroxide and a screwy idea. Ferguson laughed when 22 bleached blonde football players boarded the bus for New York the next morning.

When the Weevils reached the Big Apple, they found themselves splashed across the pages of *Collier's*. The November 23 edition had hit the newsstands early and included Kyle Crichton's lengthy article along with Hans Von Groenhof's photos. Ferguson and the players each bought multiple copies.

At a time when the world is pretty strange at best, Crichton's story began, we have to get the Arkansas Aggies in addition. We've had football teams that did this and football teams that did that, but this is the first one that considers the season a wreck if it wins a game. Its coach, Mr. Stewart A. Ferguson, has only one principle in filling his position; he refuses to coach. The squad has solved the problem of practice sessions by having no practice sessions. Their offensive is strictly impromptu, being based generally on a whim and concocted by the loudest yeller in the huddle. On the theory that a running attack needs blockers and blockers are likely to get wounded, they have no running attack . . . And yet they are one of the best attractions in football. These fabulous gentlemen from the Ozarks have taken some philosopher at his word. Football is meant to be played for fun, said this sage, and the Boll Weevils of Monticello, Arkansas, jumped on this with both feet.

The Weevils also found themselves featured in several New York newspapers and from coast-to-coast thanks to *Washington Herald* cartoonist John Hix and his syndicated "Strange as it Seems" cartoon. Hix dubbed them "the Screw-Boll Weevils."

The *New York Post* published a lengthy article on the Weevils before their game with Hofstra.

The Boll Weevils, who have carved themselves a national reputation as the Marx Brothers of football, form their own plays in the huddle, even if they've never tried them before. Every game finds them surprising Stew Ferguson, their coach, with plays he's never seen before, even in nightmares.

The *Nassau Daily Review-Star* of Long Island reported:

Our interest lies chiefly in Coach Ferguson, whose philosophy will probably go down in history as the most unique contribution ever made to college football . . . From an educational standpoint, Ferguson's plan has been lauded by authorities throughout the country. Football becomes a thrilling experience to the Arkansas boys. Win, lose or tie, pleasure in playing the games is stressed.

As the players made their way through Times Square to catch the subway to Long Island, they attracted curious onlookers, many who had read the news reports and saw Arkansas A&M scrawled across equipment bags.

Long Island in November turned out to be no place for a bunch of southern boys. A raw afternoon wind whipped across the island from the Atlantic Ocean sending a collective shiver through the players as soon as they came out of the dressing room. The Weevils were no match for a well-coached Hofstra team, losing 30-14, but managed to entertain the crowd with a number of zany plays involving passes and multiple laterals that usually lost yardage. The team's spirits were dampened by the loss of Pete Cheshier, who suffered a separated shoulder and was treated at a local hospital, but Hofstra officials paid his medical bill, relieving Ferguson of at least one financial worry.

The loss of the bus and the cost of bus tickets had put a serious dent in Ferguson's travel budget and he wondered if he had enough funds left to feed and house the team as it began the last leg of the trip, a long journey to Springfield, Missouri and a Thanksgiving morning game with Missouri State Teachers.

The Weevils spent Saturday night and all day Sunday in New York. After the game, Ferguson turned them loose in Manhattan, then slipped off to Harlem to take in a girly show at the Paradise Night Club. Ferguson didn't see as much as he had hoped to see. A week earlier, the police had raided the place and forced the girls to cover certain strategic areas of their anatomy.

Sunday evening, November 17, the boys boarded another bus headed west and most of the players slept through the night. Tunis Bishop wasn't sleepy, so he struck up a conversation with a young coal miner and his blonde, but not-so-bright wife. Ferguson, who was dozing a couple of rows in front, overheard some of the conversation, including something about wife trading. He smiled to himself and went to sleep. Bishop was a wise-cracking joker and Ferguson knew better than to take him seriously.

Apparently, the coal miner did.

When the bus stopped in Pittsburg, Bishop slid into the seat next to Ferguson. "Gosh coach, I'm in a mess. I was just fooling with a fellow and he traded me his wife for one of our parkas. Now, he's gone with the coat, and the silly wife is following me around. What'll I do?"

Ferguson stepped off the bus to talk to the woman and assured her that her husband would come back for her. "I like *him*," she said, pointing at Bishop. He could do worse, Ferguson thought, as he studied the girl's curves, then turned and walked back to the bus.

When the Weevils reached St. Louis Tuesday morning, all Ferguson had left was pocket change. He wired C. C. Smith for more money, then treated the players to their best meal in days.

As they made their way to Springfield Wednesday morning, Ferguson surveyed his team. Cheshier was out so he would have to find a quarterback. Many of the boys were sick, brought on by lack of sleep, poor food and the nasty weather they'd encountered on Long Island. When they stopped for a cup of coffee, Ferguson asked the assembled players if there was a quarterback among them. John Cubage raised his hand. The Fordyce freshman was now the Weevils' starting signal caller.

Ferguson always looked forward to spending time in Springfield. The people were friendly, the accommodations were always amenable and the food was good. Missouri Teachers was undefeated and had already been crowned champions of the Missouri Intercollegiate Athletic Association, and weren't about to let a perfect season slip away at the hands of a bunch of football pranksters.

The Bears won easily, 34-0, but the Weevils still managed to put on a show and Cubage even completed a few passes.

All that was left of the 1940 season was a final home game against Northwest Mississippi Junior College on November 27. For the second year in a row, the Weevils handled their Mississippi opponent with ease, winning 28-0. Somehow, the Weevils had managed to win two of their 11 games, prompting Ferguson to make sure he didn't schedule either the South Dakota School of Mines or Northwest Mississippi in the future. "If they can't beat us, they don't deserve to play us," Ferguson reasoned.

To Ferguson, the 1940 season was all the justification he needed for his strange football experiment. His boys had not only seen the Grand Canyon, Painted Desert and redwood forests, they had twice crossed the Rocky Mountains and visited Death Valley, Lassen Volcanic National Park, Mount Shasta, several Indian Reservations, the Mormon Temple, Mount Rushmore and the Badlands. They had explored Mammoth Cave, the Federal Treasury at Fort Knox, Fort Sumpter and toured the homes of George Washington, Abraham Lincoln, Andrew Jackson, Thomas Jefferson and Robert E. Lee.

His country boys from southeast Arkansas had played games in 12 different states, seen the nation from coast to coast and been written up in more than 400 newspapers by some of the nation's leading sport writers. Millions of American sports fans were now aware of the strange football experiment taking place at Arkansas A&M.

Ferguson explained his reasoning best in *The Long Island Daily Review-Star: "In a number of ways, we have the most unique football program being offered at the present time. It has been far more successful than our highest expectations and I really believe that we are giving our players more lasting values as a result of their playing than any other institution. However, regardless of the values, I assure you that no coach nor football team has as much fun playing the game as we do."*

CHAPTER 17

FOOTBALL FOLLIES

By the summer of 1941, much of the world was at war and most Americans assumed it was only a matter of time before U.S. soldiers joined the fray. On July 1, the U.S. registered more than 750,000 21-year-olds for the draft while the Japanese conscripted more than a million young men into military service.

Two stories dominated the newspaper headlines that summer – Hitler's march on Moscow and Joe DiMaggio's pursuit of Wee Willie Keeler's major league baseball record for hitting safely in 44 straight games. By the time the Yankee centerfielder had stretched the record to an astonishing 56 games, Les Brown and his Band of Renown had Americans tapping their feet to a catchy new tune, *Joltin' Joe DiMaggio*. In Boston, a skinny outfielder named Ted Williams was trying to become the first player in 17 years to bat .400.

Many of the boys who played for Arkansas A&M in 1939 and 1940 joined the National Guard unit on campus and by summer had been called to active duty in Alaska. The missing boys included most of Ferguson's better players.

Buddy Carson spent the summer trying to get a job as a civilian flight instructor. He had learned to fly in A&M's Civil Air Patrol program and had a pilot's license, but at 20, was considered too young to be an instructor. "Son, you passed everything, but you're too damn young," his supervisor told him. "You'll be younger than nearly all your students."

In early September, Carson enlisted in the Army Air Corps, but since he was still a student, was allowed to return to school and the football team.

It wasn't much of a team.

In 1939 and '40, the Boll Weevils had enough football talent to be competitive when they played it straight. They had to work hard to lose some of their games and still managed to win three times in spite of themselves. That wouldn't be a problem in '41.

Ferguson's squad was so depleted that the *Arkansas Democrat* reported (with tongue firmly in cheek) that A&M's spring practice consisted of "jumping on the college bus and riding around campus. There were no injuries."

The 1941 schedule would keep the Boll Weevils on the road for stretches of 22 and 30 days at a time with no home games until the season finale against Magnolia A&M. They would travel the country in a new bus, with Joe Coker at the wheel.

THE 1941 BOLL WEEVIL SCHEDULE

Sept.	19	Louisiana College	Pineville, Louisiana
Sept.	25	Mars Hill College	Asheville, North Carolina
Sept.	27	Appalachian State	Boone, North Carolina
Oct.	8	Spring Hill College	Mobile, Alabama
Oct.	11	North Texas State	Denton, Texas
Oct.	27	Bradley Tech*	Peoria, Illinois
Oct.	30	Moravian College	Bethlehem, Pennsylvania
Nov.	1	Upsala College	East Orange, New Jersey
Nov.	7	St. Francis College	Johnstown, Pennsylvania

Nov.	10	Davis & Elkins College	Davis, West Virginia
Nov.	19	Evansville	Evansville, Indiana
Nov.	26	Magnolia A&M	Monticello, Arkansas

*(Originally scheduled for October 4, but rescheduled after heavy rains made the field unplayable.)

Ferguson had scheduled 12 games when most teams played no more than nine or 10. Included were brutal stretches that included two games in three days and (thanks to rescheduling) three games in six days.

Missing from the '41 schedule were the South Dakota School of Mines and Northwest Mississippi Junior College, teams A&M had beaten the previous season. Ferguson dropped them because, as he told one sportswriter, "those teams apparently didn't take football seriously enough if they can lose to us." Secretly, Ferguson was hoping for a "perfect" season – perfect in this case meaning 0-12.

Ferguson considered this latest team his worst. Seven members of the squad had never played a down of competitive football. The boys with the most experience, and who would usually comprise the starting lineup, included ends Jimmy "Twig" Moore of Gould and gangly 6-foot-7 Lawrence "The Stork" Lavender of Star City; tackles Paul Stegall of Monticello and Arthur Isch of McGehee, guards Bob Potter and Bill Bowers, both of Lamar, Missouri; center Oscar Dove of El Dorado; halfbacks Pete McDonald of Gillett and George Heroman of Monticello; fullback John Scritchfield of El Dorado; and quarterbacks Benny Gaston of McGehee, and Carson, who would also see action at fullback, and along with Red England, serve as the team's punter.

One of the team's new players was Lester "Yank" Corwin, a native of Long Island, New York (hence the nickname) who, after watching the Weevils the previous year at Hofstra, decided to hitchhike to Monticello and join in the silliness.

J. P. Leveritt would reprise his role as Ferguson's assistant coach and trainer and would occasionally insert himself into games if the situation called for it.

The squad resembled a high school team, Ferguson thought. The players averaged 163 pounds and a month over 18 years old. They were smaller than the team at Monticello High School and, Ferguson suspected, younger as well.

One of the newcomers, Bix Stillwell, was an accomplished drummer who had never played football. He earned playing time at halfback and stunned both Ferguson and his teammates by scoring the first time he touched the ball in a game.

This group of Boll Weevils would have to rely almost solely on comedy because they weren't going to entertain anyone with their football skill. The Weevils would certainly look funny. Ferguson made sure of that by obtaining several boxes of new jerseys – salesmen's samples – in a rainbow of colors. The players could choose from black, purple, blue, red, white, green, orange, yellow, gold, or brown and in a variety of styles. They also had their "official" green and yellow jerseys purchased two years earlier. When they took the field, the Weevils often appeared to have spent the night in a paint store that had been hit by a tornado. If they felt like changing jerseys at halftime, that was okay with Ferguson. One of the Weevils' favorite ploys in '41 involved changing into jerseys the same color as their opponents before coming back on the field for the third quarter.

The Weevils practiced just four times before opening the season with a 60-0 loss to Louisiana College that involved the usual clowning. One of the new boys playing his first game made a tackle shortly after being put in the game, then proceeded to tackle anything that moved, including his own players and the officials. "Coach," he told Ferguson as he came off the field, "I just got the feel of tackling and had to tackle everything I saw." Ferguson later viewed him as the team's best defender.

Four days later, the Weevils left on a 22-day trip that would take them from North Carolina to Canada. First stop was Asheville, North Carolina and a game with Mars Hill College.

For two years, Ferguson and his team had received mostly favorable press as they traveled the country, but when they reached Asheville, they encountered a reporter from the *Asheville Citizen* who thought football too serious an endeavor to be mocked. After the Weevils played quite respectably in a 19-0 loss, the paper described their play as *"almost as funny as a crutch"* and said they had *"disappointed a turnout of about 1,000 customers . . . It was the consensus of opinion that the Aggies would do better to stick to real football and quit trying to please the fans with comedy."*

The next day, Benny Gaston read the ill-tempered story and approached Ferguson in tears. "Coach, we're so rotten that I guess we'd better try to pay our own expenses for the rest of the trip," said Gaston. The rest of the boys had read the paper and, Ferguson thought, were hopelessly depressed. Ferguson was livid and stayed that way until the team reached Boone, North Carolina. The Weevils had just one day between their games with Mars Hill and Appalachian State and Ferguson was concerned about both the physical and emotional well-being of his players.

The students at Appalachian State took care of that. When the Weevils pulled up to the university's field house, they were ushered inside to a rousing ovation as the guests at a two-hour pep rally. Some of the Weevils sat in with the Appalachian State band or joined the cheerleaders on stage. It was one of the wildest student gatherings Ferguson had ever seen, and it got wilder when Bix Stillwell commandeered a drum set and began entertaining.

The game was no contest with Appalachian State winning 67-0. The boys tried to put on a show but still didn't have their hearts in it after being ridiculed in the newspaper. About the only comedy the boys experienced came in the form of a sign hanging over a toilet in their dressing room:

It ain't no use to stand on the seat,
These mountain crabs can jump 40 feet.

After the game, Ferguson was still despondent over the treatment of his players by the Asheville paper when he was summoned from his dressing room by Appalachian State President B. B. Dougherty. The white-haired Dougherty had been president of Appalachian State since 1899 and appeared feeble to Ferguson until he grabbed the coach's hand. "I wish I were president of a college that turned out football teams like yours," Dougherty told a stunned Ferguson.

"But we played so rotten this afternoon," Ferguson answered, "and did you read what they said about us in Asheville?"

"Of course, of course," said Dougherty. "That's one of the reasons I came down here to see you this afternoon. Your boys have had two bad punches, but they're still the kind of boys that I'd like to have in my college."

Ferguson thanked Dougherty, allowing that his team still wasn't any good.

"You're wrong," Dougherty said. "You have the finest bunch of boys I've ever seen play football. I'd sure like to trade you our touchdowns for your boys. You're plenty fine people."

Ferguson passed along Dougherty's praise to his team and both coach and players left North Carolina with their spirits buoyed. The Weevils were scheduled to play Bradley Tech in Peoria, Illinois on October 4 so they headed north on what would be a roundabout journey. They stopped for the night in Bristol, Virginia where Ferguson went to a drug store to buy medicine. Most of his players were sick with colds and Ferguson spent much of the night administering cold remedies.

A long trip through Kentucky brought them to Cincinnati by nightfall. The boys toured the Queen City the next morning before driving to Dayton for a short work-out at the University of Dayton's football stadium, then it was off to Detroit, arriving late on the evening of September 29. Rather than go immediately to a hotel, Ferguson decided it would be fun to let the boys stand on foreign soil so he directed Coker to drive the bus across the bridge separating Detroit from Windsor, Ontario.

Canadian immigration officials took a look at the bus and decided the Wandering Weevils were no threat to the continued good relations between the United States and Canada and let them cross.

The next day, the Weevils headed to Ann Arbor and another practice session at the University of Michigan. As the bus pulled to a stop on campus, Fritz Crisler stuck his head in the door. "Damn, it looks like there's some football players in here," Crisler boomed. "Anybody want to sign up for Michigan?"

Crisler was already a coaching legend, winning national championships at Princeton in 1933 and '35 before becoming Michigan's head coach in 1938. It was Crisler who introduced the distinctive winged helmet that forever became identified with Wolverine football. Crisler escorted Ferguson and the boys on a tour of Michigan's imposing field house, a structure that would one day carry Crisler's name. The players gawked at a building like none they had ever seen, then got dressed, went outdoors and held a work-out on Michigan's practice field. The *Ann Arbor News* sent a reporter and photographer to cover the practice and the Weevils were happy to demonstrate their unorthodox formations and plays, including the Swinging Gate. Three photographs and a lengthy story appeared in the next day's paper, including a photo of J. P. Leveritt suspended upside down in the air as he practiced handsprings while holding a football.

From Michigan it was on to South Bend and another visit to Notre Dame. Ferguson and the players paid their respects at the grave of Knute Rockne, walked the campus and met briefly with new Irish coach Frank Leahy before heading to Chicago. The Weevils spent the next two days touring the Windy City before boarding the bus for Peoria and the game with Bradley Tech.

An hour before game time, a cloudburst turned into a flash flood, dumping sheets of rain on the freshly sod playing surface at Bradley Stadium, forcing Bradley officials to cancel the game. When a Bradley representative tried to hand Ferguson a $500 check for the minimum game guarantee, Ferguson wouldn't accept it. "We'll come back and play you at a future date when we can really earn that check," Ferguson said. They eventually agreed to re-schedule the contest for October 27. In the meantime, the Weevils had games to play in Mobile, Alabama and Denton, Texas before they could return to Illinois.

CHAPTER 18

TIME CAPSULE

If one game could be summoned to tell football historians what the Wandering Weevils were all about, it might have been their game with North Texas State in Denton, Texas on October 11, 1941.

It belongs in a time capsule.

Before reaching Denton, the Weevils headed south from Illinois to Alabama for a game in Mobile with Spring Hill College. The press in Mobile was glowing with praise for the Weevils and invited fans to come see "slap-happy football."

Arkansas A&M, the school where football is played for fun, makes a one-night stand here Wednesday night at Murphy high field against the Spring Hill Badgers and it is a stand that no football fan should miss. The visitors, known by the title of 'Wandering Boll Weevils,' is (sic) easily the most color-ful aggregation – collegiate, professional or prep – in the na-tion. Their color has made them one of the most widely-known small-name teams in the country.

The Weevils didn't disappoint, pulling out their usual tricks while absorbing a 37-0 beating. The boys did handsprings with the ball, rode into and out of the game on a bicycle and climbed into the grandstand to visit with the fans. From there, it was on to Denton and the last leg of a 22-day journey. North Texas coach Jack Sisco was reportedly preparing his team for any contingency, but even he couldn't have envisioned what transpired that day.

It started on the opening kickoff. While Ferguson sat in the stands next to an attractive coed, the players grabbed her boyfriend, a North Texas cheerleader, gave him a jersey and a helmet and forced him to kick off. They grabbed another cheerleader and made her the coach, which worked until she started putting her arm around each player as he came off the field, making it impossible to keep the boys interested in playing. The "coach" was summarily fired.

At one point, facing a fourth down on their own eight-yard line, the Weevils came to the line of scrimmage, and with the exception of the center, turned their backs to the North Texas defense. Oscar Dove snapped the ball to Benny Gaston, who was promptly tackled by his own teammates before the North Texas defenders could get to him.

When North Texas lined up for an extra point attempt following one of many touchdowns, the Weevils didn't bother to rush the kicker, instead falling on their faces. The distracted kicker missed.

At halftime, a bored Ferguson caught a cab to downtown Denton and settled into a diner for a hamburger and cup of coffee. When he returned to the game near the end of the third quarter, his players were outfitted in dark green jerseys the same as North Texas. They had changed in the dressing room. The only players on the field were those in the game. The rest of the Weevils were in the stands chatting with the North Texas coeds. John Scritchfield had cornered a particularly attractive red-head.

Early in the second half, Lawrence Lavender entered the game wearing a tall silk hat and bob-tailed dress coat over his uniform. A student manager followed dressed as Lavender's valet. At one point, all 11 Weevils on the field stood at attention with helmets removed while a North Texas ball carrier scored.

Sisco became so disgusted he sent most of his varsity players to the showers before the fourth quarter started and played mostly freshmen for the final 15 minutes. After the game, a 60-0 North Texas win, Ferguson was approached by Francis X. Tolbert of the *Fort Worth Star-Telegram*. "I have been coaching the Boll Weevils for four seasons," Ferguson told Tolbert, "and I can safely say that this is my worst team."

Tolbert's game story, under the headline "Worst of All the Boll Weevils Holds North Texas to 60-0!," began with *Old Arkansas A&M took it on the chin again here Friday night. The 23 zanies who form A&M's football team gleefully absorbed a 60-0 whipping at the hands of the North Texas State Eagles . . . Except for the scoreless fourth quarter, by which time the Eagles' disgusted mentor, Jack Sisco, had sent most of his athletes to the showers, the Boll Weevils put up little more resistance than so many blocking dummies. In fact, dummies might have done better. Anyway, they wouldn't have traitorously tackled their own ballcarriers.*

In the dressing room after the game, a North Texas professor burst through the door, eager to shake Ferguson's hand. The excited professor was almost shouting as he praised Ferguson as "the greatest man in the history of football" and a man worthy of having a monument erected in his honor.

When Ferguson passed that bit of news on to C. C. Smith, the A&M business manager allowed that Ferguson already had plenty of monuments in his honor in every cow and horse pasture in the country.

The Weevils returned to Monticello for a few days, just long enough to go to class a few times, do their laundry and pick up some clean shirts before leaving on a 30-day journey that would take them as far as New England and burnish their reputation as the goofiest football team in history.

The Weevils had 16 days between their game with North Texas and their next game with Bradley Tech on Monday, October 27, which left plenty of time for rest and a little sightseeing. They would need the rest. The Weevils were scheduled to play three games in six days.

It was raining again when they reached Peoria, but the Bradley field was in good enough shape to play. Inspired by their antics at North Texas, the Weevils were at their zany best. During pre-game warm-ups, some of the players carried a bat and ball onto the field and played an impromptu baseball game.

In the second quarter, with the ball on their own 43-yard line, the Weevils came to the line of scrimmage, and as they did at North Texas, turned their backs to the Bradley defense. As the Bradley players stood up laughing, Dove again snapped the ball to Gaston, who turned and raced toward his own goal line, only to be tackled short of the end zone by his own players as the crowd of 3,000 howled with laughter.

Prior to the game, the players had managed to secure some cheap umbrellas and used them as they rode bicycles into and out of the huddle. On defense, the Weevils played anything from two- to 11-man lines. When Lawrence Lavender made the mistake of gaining ground, he was dragged to the sideline where his teammates pretended to beat him senseless. Bix Stillwell thrilled the crowd by climbing into the stands to play the drums with the Bradley band.

Ferguson watched all this, first from the grandstands, then from the press box, and later from the Bradley sideline. At half-time, some of the Weevils stayed on the field and practiced place-kicking in to the grandstands to the delight of the fans.

Yank Corwin reprised Lavender's role as a gentleman, entering the game in a long coat and derby hat. When he reached the huddle, his teammates pelted him with balls of mud from the wet field. As the Braves attempted a point-after, the Weevils lounged on the ground and the crowd roared when the kick failed. The Weevils argued with officials about the legality of running down a Bradley ball carrier while riding a bike. They formed three-man high pyramids on defense, and, after catching a Braves ball carrier, waltzed with him to the end zone. The stadium's public address announcer complimented the Weevils on their Southern courtesy.

Each time Bradley scored, Weevil substitutes would race to the end zone and tie a dark pink balloon that looked like a loaf of bologna to the crossbar of the goalposts.

Trailing 67-0 in the game's fading minutes, the Weevils mounted a drive that covered 50 yards. Most of the crowd was still there and began chanting "We want a touchdown" as the Weevils neared the goal line only to lose the ball on downs at the four. When the game ended, a group of Bradley fans invited Ferguson to a party in his honor that lasted until 5:00 the next morning.

Russell Perry of the *Peoria Journal-Transcript*, summed up the game with a clever lede:

> *Fighting valiantly the last figment of their collective imagination, the football juggernuts of Arkansas A and M college went down under Bradley's Braves in the last 60 minutes of play last night before a well-entertained though somewhat chilled crowd of 3,000 at the Stadium.*

The next day, the Weevils boarded their bus and headed east to Bethlehem, Pa., and a game with the Moravian Greyhounds. Two hard days of travel brought A&M to Bethlehem shortly before midnight Wednesday, giving the Weevils only a few hours rest before their Thursday night game. The Weevils had received plenty of publicity following their antics at North Texas and Bradley Tech and an overflow crowd of 4,000 crowded into Moravian Stadium to see if the newspaper accounts were true.

The Boll Weevils didn't disappoint the paying customers, flinging the ball all over the field and poking fun at Moravian, recording their touchdowns by again hanging balloons that resembled bologna from the crossbars each time the Greyhounds scored. Three grinning players were captured in a photo that appeared on the front page of the sports section of the next day's *Bethlehem Globe-Times* headlined "It's 'Baloney' to 'Boll Weevils'".

At times the Boll Weevils had the spectators hysterical with laughter, said the newspaper, but in spite of the comedy, played good football in spots.

Following the 33-0 loss, Ferguson and the Weevils found a visitor waiting for them in their dressing room. Bob Meyer was the young, first-year coach of Upsala College, the Weevils next opponent on Saturday in Montclair, N.J. Meyer had come to scout Arkansas A&M and had an unusual request.

Meyer wanted to address the Weevils and encourage their best effort against his winless team. "I want you guys to get in there and fight," Meyer said, as Ferguson fell off his coaching stool. "Play to win as you've never played before." Meyer explained that he didn't want to win his first game by having the opposition hand it to him.

Ferguson was stunned. "That's the first time any coach ever asked us to try to beat his team," he told reporters. Impressed by Meyer, Ferguson promised to "shoot the works" although "the boys will get sore and refuse to play" without at least a little clowning.

The *New York Post* noted the Weevils' arrival in New Jersey, praising Ferguson and his team for "blowing away the clouds of commercial clap-trap that obscure the original purpose of an essentially simple sport involving the carrying and throwing of a wind-bag."

Ferguson kept his word to Meyer, instructing his players to temper their comedy act and play real football. Had the game been played in better weather conditions and on a dry field, the Boll Weevils might have won. Gaston and Carson combined to complete 21 passes, including a 34-yard pass from Gaston to Stillwell that briefly tied the score at 6-6 in the first quarter. It was A&M's first touchdown – and first points of any kind – of the season after seven straight shutouts. The Weevils confined their clowning to the sidelines, taking their shoes off and diving into puddles or climbing into the stands.

"America's nuttiest football team, the Arkansas Aggies, turned out to be not so crazy yesterday," said the *Newark Sunday Call. "They had Upsala trembling in its cleats before the East Orange eleven finally got rolling and sloshed through a 19-6 victory . . . Had the field been dry, the Aggies might have scored their first victory . . ."*

With their "perfect" season still intact, the Weevils loaded up the bus and headed to Manhattan and their usual digs at the Times Square Hotel. Ferguson gave the boys enough money for three days of sightseeing and turned them loose. He wouldn't see them together as a group for three days.

The *New York Post* let its readers know the Wandering Weevils were in town:

THE BOLL WEEVILS ARE HERE: Arkansas A&M, the Marx Brothers of football, may be viewed at the Times Square Hotel until tomorrow morning . . .

Ferguson and a few of the boys took part in a photo shoot for *Newsweek* magazine. Some of the players conserved their money but most were broke by the time the three days were over. Benny Gaston and J. P. Leveritt, however, came back with their pockets full of cash. Gaston had spotted a notice on the hotel bulletin board. The Munsingwear Company was looking for male underwear models. Gaston, Leveritt and several of their teammates applied and Gaston and Leveritt got the job, posing for a series of photos in their underwear. The photos would appear in the December issue of *Life* magazine.

When their tour of New York was over, Ferguson took the team to New Haven, Connecticut to visit Yale University. Eli Coach Spike Nelson invited the Weevils to practice on Yale's field, then watch his team practice. By the time they had eaten a large and expensive dinner, Ferguson was growing short on funds. Rather than stay at a hotel in New Haven, he decided to save money and ordered Coker to start driving west. They would cross the Hudson River upstream from New York City and bunk at some small country inn. As they drove into the rural Hudson Valley, Ferguson stared into the night and let his imagination get the best of him. Recalling Washington Irving's *Legend of Sleepy Hollow*, Ferguson began to imagine the headless horseman pursuing Ichabod Crane. When they pulled into a small tourist resort at the base of a mountain, Ferguson thought the proprietor and his assistant looked sinister. When they offered to let the team stay at any price Ferguson wanted to pay, he shooed the boys back on the bus and ordered Coker to find a city – any city – with lots of people around. The players just shrugged. By now, nothing Stewart Ferguson did could surprise them.

The Weevils arrived at the Hotel Waldo in Middletown, Pennsylvania at 2 a.m., and thanks to the good graces of a St. Francis College supporter, were able to stay there for three days at a bargain rate. The game with St. Francis was scheduled for Sunday afternoon in Johnstown and Ferguson pleaded with his boys not to tell their families and friends back home that they had played a game on Sunday. The game itself was brutal. A&M's opponents usually played along with the Weevils' clowning, but occasionally, a serious opponent would become disgusted with the antics and try to inflict as much damage as possible.

St. Francis was undefeated and in no mood for laughs. By the game's conclusion, after the Red Flash had recorded a 59-6 win, most of the Weevils were limping, battered and bruised. That didn't stop the boys from attending a lavish dinner in their honor that evening at the St. Francis student union. The Weevil players, many of them from tee-totaling Southern Baptist families, were wide-eyed as each table was served large quantities of wine. Not only had they played a football game on Sunday, they were openly enjoying the fruit of the vine. Ferguson again made his players promise to keep the episode to themselves.

CHAPTER 19

THREE GAMES LEFT

Three games remained on the 1941 schedule – a November 15 date with Davis & Elkins College in Elkins, West Virginia, a November 19 game at Evansville, Indiana, and a season-ending home game against traditional rival Magnolia A&M on Thanksgiving Day, November 26. The players were blithely unaware of trouble brewing in the Pacific and most had never heard of a remote naval base called Pearl Harbor.

Ferguson and his team, still bruised and battered from their brawl with St. Francis, eased into Philadelphia for a sightseeing excursion. The Weevils had 12 days to kill before their next game and would need the time to heal their wounded. Ferguson even considered cancelling the remainder of the schedule and taking his team home.

The boys seemed to bounce back during a tour of historical sites in Philadelphia. They saw the Liberty Bell and Independence Hall, and when the tour guide wasn't looking, sat in George Washington's chair. While the players watched an Armistice Day Parade, Ferguson went in search of a doctor for Fuzzy Watts, who injured an already bum leg at St. Francis. Years earlier, Watts' leg was badly crushed in an accident, requiring skin grafts that had broken open during the St. Francis game.

Without an appointment, Ferguson searched for several hours before locating an elderly doctor with a thick German accent. The doctor repaired the torn skins grafts and blood vessels in Watts' leg, then asked Ferguson for three dollars. Ferguson gratefully pressed a ten dollar bill into the doctor's hand.

The Weevils spent two days in Philadelphia and one in Baltimore before heading to Washington. Ferguson contacted Congressman Francis Case of South Dakota, an old friend from their days at Dakota Wesleyan, and Case arranged for the boys to view a session of the House of Representatives.

By the time the Weevils arrived in West Virginia, the walking wounded had healed enough, not only to play, but to put on a memorable show. Midway through the first half, with Ferguson watching from the press box, a group of players grabbed a sideline microphone and brought the house down by singing a boisterous rendition of "You Are My Sunshine."

Later, with Davis & Elkins threatening to score, J. P. Leveritt inserted himself into the game at end. At the snap of the ball, Leveritt slid to his right, keeping a close eye on the opposing quarterback, who was tucked behind a convoy of two blockers. As the three players approached, Leveritt leaped over the blockers from a flat-footed stance, landing on the startled quarterback and dragging him to the ground short of the goal line. Flags flew but the officials weren't sure what to call. Leveritt had not been offside and had not used another player to catapult himself over the blockers. After a lengthy conference between the officials and a heated argument from the A&M players, the referee finally turned to Leveritt and said, "Son, you just can't do that," and penalized the Weevils. The 41-0 loss kept the perfect season intact at 0-10.

As the Weevils boarded their bus for a meandering trip through Ohio, a half a world away, submarines of the Japanese Imperial

Navy left Tokyo Bay for the Hawaiian Islands as the vanguard of a
secret task force.

The Weevils arrived in Evansville, Indiana on Friday, November
21, a day before their game with the Evansville Purple Aces, and
held a brief work-out at Enlow Field. While the players practiced,
Ferguson went downtown to watch a movie. The next afternoon,
with Ferguson watching from the grandstands, the Weevils were at
their slap-stick best and thrilled an overflow crowd that braved wet
conditions to watch a team they'd been reading about for days in
the local papers. The Weevils made their entrance to the stadium in
their usual unorthodox fashion. Enlow Field was surrounded by a
tall chain-link fence, and rather than come through the open gate,
the players climbed up and over the fence.

Once inside, the Weevils used cheap umbrellas to perform re-
hearsed skits. Lawrence Lavender walked imperiously onto the field
dressed in a top hat, starched white shirt and tuxedo jacket over his
uniform, accompanied by a student manager "valet" holding an umbrella. Extending his 6-foot-7 frame to its tallest, Lavender stretched
out a white-gloved hand and presented referee Bud Pointer with a
white card engraved with Lavender's name. With as much flourish as
he could muster, Lavender removed his coat, shirt and hat, handed
them to his valet and inserted himself into the backfield where he
immediately carried the ball for a nice gain.

Pointer joined in the spirit of the game, watching the Weevils
diagram a play in the mud, then telling the Evansville defense it
was going to be a pass. "Yeah," said Benny Gaston. "We're going to
pass to that guy," pointing at Pete McDonald. The pass was complete for a 30-yard gain.

Early in the second quarter, a drunk wobbled out of the stands
and made his way to the A&M sideline where he was welcomed by
the players as a coach. The imposter got to keep his job until a reporter found Ferguson in the stands and told him that most of the fans

thought the drunk was really A&M's coach. Ferguson decided it might be a good idea to clear up the confusion, making his way to the press box, where he introduced himself over the stadium loudspeaker. Two policemen whisked the drunk away while a third told Ferguson that they had hesitated because they didn't want to arrest the visiting coach.

Jimmy Fraser, writing for *The Sunday Courier and Press* of Evansville, summed up the game:

Football reached the heights (or depths) of idiocy in Evansville yesterday as the Evansville College Purple Aces, in between guffaws, downed the droll, screw-Boll Weevils from Arkansas A&M College 26 to 6.

Now 0-11, the Weevils boarded their bus and headed back to Arkansas and the end of a 30-day journey. When they reached Monticello, Coker circled the campus loop three times, horn blaring, to let the students know they were home.

Three days later, on Thursday, November 26, 1941, the Wandering Weevils suited up for their season finale against old rival Magnolia A&M. Most of the fans were still feeling the effects of their Thanksgiving dinner as the Weevils trotted on to the field dressed in a wide array of uniforms. As the two teams lined up for their 2 p.m. kickoff, A&M's Bill Bowers came sprinting out of the locker room, equipment bag in hand. As the fans howled, Bowers reached in the bag, pulled out his jersey and put it on.

Bowers, who doubled as the kick-off man, placed the ball at the 40-yard line, then started back . . . and back . . . and back. Bowers retreated to his own goal line, then began a pell-mell sprint toward the ball before purposely tripping and falling flat on his face five yards short of his objective while another player kicked the ball.

During the game, benchwarmers amused themselves by driving a horse and cart around the field, mocking the Magnolia mascot, the Mulerider. When one of the Weevils was accidentally disabled, four teammates picked him up, dragged him to the sideline and tried to revive him. They offered prayers to Allah, then covered him with a sheet, leaving the rest to fate. A&M's usual foolishness resulted in a 25-7 loss, completing a "perfect" 0-12 season.

As the players left the field, only the seniors knew they had played their last football game. Buddy Carson still had two seasons of eligibility remaining, but at the moment had other things on his mind. Immediately after the game, Carson and his girlfriend, Elloise, jumped in a friend's car and drove to nearby McGehee to get married.

On the other side of the world, at a naval base in northern Japan, a strike force of six aircraft carriers loaded with more than 400 attack aircraft and accompanied by dozens of support vessels, left Japanese waters for Pearl Harbor.

The Wandering Weevils made the national news one more time, appearing in the December 1, 1941, issue of *Newsweek*. A photo showed Ferguson at the team hotel engaged in a strategy session with five of his players. Carson appeared to be the only one paying attention while Ralph Stegall sat, chin resting in his hand daydreaming while three more players huddled behind Ferguson under an umbrella.

If Minnesota was the best team of 1941, the article began, what was the worst? Probably the Arkansas A&M Boll Weevils, a group of barnstormers who have no intention of winning, but instead try to see how much fun eleven men can have playing football. Their meanderings by bus over most of the United States are really for educational purposes; football pays the freight . . . So far the Weevils have lost every game, scoring 18 points to their opponents' 493. But they've had their fun on their long ramble, which wound up against Evansville (Ind.) College last Saturday. They lost by a close score: 26-6, with some of the players carrying umbrellas. And this week, the wandering Weevils return home to classes — if the self-respecting citizens of Monticello, Ark., will let them inside the city limits.

Stewart Ferguson left Arkansas A&M in 1942 and there would be no more Wandering Weevils. In fact, there would be no football at all at Arkansas A&M that year. With most of the young men in military service, enrollment fell so low the future of the college was in doubt. Marvin Bankston saved the day by persuading the Navy to place a V-12 officer training program on the A&M campus. By 1943, the campus was awash in able-bodied officer candidates, many of them former football players.

When the University of Arkansas called A&M in early September searching for an opponent to begin the '43 season, the brigade commander called his students together. How many had played football? Most of the unit stepped forward. How many had played college football? Again, a large percentage of the unit stepped forward.

With one week to practice, the players borrowed a football from Monticello High School, drew up a hand full of plays, then boarded a bus for Fayetteville. Without uniforms or equipment, they borrowed helmets and road jerseys from the UA, trotted onto the turf at Razorback Stadium – and won 20-12. That might have been A&M's only game in 1943, but when the Naval Air Technical Training Command (NATTC) team at Millington, Tenn., near Memphis had its football season suspended due to Navy regulations A&M assumed their schedule and uniforms, playing their home games at Crump Stadium in Memphis. They called themselves the Arkansas A&M Aggies, eschewing the official boll weevil mascot. The name "weevils" was too closely associated with losing and left a bad taste in the mouths of local fans. The '43 Arkansas A&M Aggies posted a 5-1-1 record and earned a spot in the Oil Bowl in Houston, Tex., forerunner of the now-defunct Bluebonnet Bowl.

The Wandering Weevil era was officially over.

There would be no more football for fun at Arkansas A&M. Stewart Ferguson had enlisted in the Navy shortly after the attack on Pearl Harbor and spent most of the war at LSU, instructing officer candidates.

Arkansas A&M became a football power in the 1950's, winning five Arkansas Intercollegiate Conference championships in six years. The Boll Weevils won four more league crowns in the '60s. In 1971, Arkansas A&M became the University of Arkansas at Monticello and won league titles in 1979 and '93 while fielding mostly competitive teams every year. Today, the Boll Weevils still play their home games in the stadium dedicated on that long-ago October day in 1934, the concrete façade still the backbone of the west grandstands, much as it was when Stewart Ferguson was coaching.

The Wandering Weevils were unique in the history of college athletics. At no time before or since has an athletic team representing a recognized college or university thumbed its nose at the time-honored tradition of playing to win. In three years, Ferguson's band of football vagabonds had been outscored 1,143 to 191, lost 30 of 33 games, traveled more than 40,000 miles . . . and enjoyed every minute of the experience.

To Stewart Ferguson, winning was irrelevant. He just wanted his players to have fun and didn't mind poking holes in the myth of the importance of sports. To understand Ferguson best is to read his own words:

"I want to be remembered by my players as a sort of fireside fool when they tell their children about the places they've been, the states they played in, and the things they learned when they played football for Arkansas A&M. I want them to say, 'That Coach Ferguson was sort of a damn fool - didn't care much whether we won or lost. But, boy! - the times we had and the things we saw."

CHAPTER 20

After the Laughter

Shortly after the attack on Pearl Harbor, most of the Wandering Weevils either enlisted or were drafted into military service. Some were already part of the campus military unit, Battery B of the Army's Second Battalion, 206th Coast Artillery, and were shipped to the Aleutian Islands in Alaska. Others enlisted or were drafted and a few were deemed physically unable to serve.

Benny Gaston, the little halfback who stripped to his jock strap against Humboldt State, became an officer in the Marine Corps and was killed in 1943 in an accident during flight training in Florida.

Boyd Arnold, the erstwhile All-American, was rejected for military service due to the residual effect of several football injuries. He became a highly successful high school coach in Arkansas, turning tiny Rison into a football powerhouse before moving to Hampton to start the football program from scratch. Arnold died in 1999 at 86.

Carleton Spears, the handsome captain of the '39 team, was flying an unarmed plane from an aircraft carrier on December 7, 1941, when he was shot down trying to land at Pearl Harbor. He survived.

Coy Brown, the sleepy-eyed lineman, had his eye condition fixed by surgery, went into the construction business and became one of the state's most successful contractors.

John Arnold went to Alaska with the 206th and later coached with Boyd Arnold at Rison. He left coaching to become a public school administrator at Kensett, Hermitage and Prairie Grove. He died in 1972 at the relatively young age of 54.

Thomas Edward "Eddie Mac" McMillan, the 137-pound guard who nearly ruined Stewart Ferguson's plans with a young teacher, was also stationed in Alaska. McMillan was one of 1,300 GI's in the Aleutian Islands when the Japanese began bombing Dutch Harbor as a feint to draw attention away from Midway Island. Had the Japanese succeeded at Midway, McMillan and his mates would have faced an invasion force of 10,000 Japanese soldiers. "If Midway hadn't gone well, they'd have got us," he remembered. McMillan was also part of the invasion of Corregidor in the Philippines and after the war, moved to Texas to work as a senior research technician for Dow Chemical. When interviewed for this book in the fall of 2010, McMillan was 92 and living on a ranch outside Brazoria, Texas. McMillan played less than one season with the Wandering Weevils but remembered the experience fondly.

J. P. Leveritt's life after football reads like the pages of *Forrest Gump*, a man always in the right place at the right time. Leveritt was accepted into the Army's physical rehabilitation program, and while most of his teammates were sent to Alaska or saw combat in other areas, Leveritt was chosen for an assignment at Walter Reed Hospital in Washington, D.C. He quickly made a name for himself at Walter Reed by creating a rehabilitation program based on the principles he had learned as a weight lifter and gymnast.

Leveritt's life changed dramatically one day in 1945 when a colonel came to Walter Reed and began asking around for anyone with experience in deep tissue massage. Leveritt had taken a semester off at Arkansas A&M to learn the art of Swedish massage and was referred to the colonel.

A few days later, the same colonel ordered Leveritt to a black sedan parked in front of the hospital and told him to get in. As they drove into the Maryland countryside, the colonel explained to Leveritt that he was being taken to the home of Secretary of War Henry Stimson. The 77-year-old Stimson was suffering from acute circulatory problems, not responding to medication and in such poor health he was unable to leave his home. Surgeon General Norman Kirk prescribed exercise and deep tissue massage as a last resort.

Numerous masseurs and physical therapists had worked on Stimson with minimal results. Leveritt gave the Secretary of War a thorough massage, starting with his fingers and limbs. The process took nearly 40 minutes and when Leveritt was finished, Stimson sat up on the table, looked at the colonel, then at Leveritt, and grinned. "Can you come back?" Stimson asked.

For the next month, a car came for Leveritt twice a week. Stimson's improvement was so dramatic that he was able to return to his office at the Pentagon and Leveritt was asked to accompany the Secretary to the Potsdam Conference in Germany to continue his treatments. At Potsdam, Leveritt had a front row seat to history as President Harry Truman, Communist Party General Secretary Josef Stalin, and British Prime Ministers Winston Churchill and Clement Atlee decided the fate of war-torn Europe.

When the conference ended, Leveritt accompanied Stimson to Berchtesgaden, Adolph Hitler's alpine hideaway, before arriving at the headquarters of General George Patton, a palatial estate once owned by a high-ranking member of the Nazi Party.

Leveritt met Patton on more than one occasion, but remembered one encounter vividly. "I was on my way down a long corridor in the mansion where we were staying," said Leveritt. "I was headed for Stimson's room when down the hall comes Patton. The corridor was lined with busts of Hitler, so Patton grabbed one, and with a big grin on his face tossed it to me as he passed. 'Here, Leveritt, give this to the Secretary. Tell him I promised to give him Hitler's head.' Stimson got a big laugh out of that."

Leveritt returned to Walter Reed, but by then his reputation had reached from the Pentagon to 1600 Pennsylvania Avenue. Leveritt was summoned to the White House where he met with Truman's doctor. As they were talking, in strode the President of the United States. "He stuck his hand out, shook my hand and said 'Welcome aboard. I'm glad they found you,'" said Leveritt.

For the next four years, Leveritt worked at the White House. He built a steam cabinet for the President, gave him massages two to three times a week, and even accompanied Truman on his famous "whistle stop" campaign in 1948.

"Truman was such a genuine person and had such a sense of humor," Leveritt said. "When he was in that steam cabinet and it was just the two of us in there, he told me some fantastic stories that I'd never repeat. I knew a lot of things going on that a lot of people never knew."

With a master's degree from George Washington University, Leveritt returned to Arkansas in 1949 where he started a weight lifting gym before heading the physical education program of a new school in North Little Rock. He spent six years as director of the YMCA in Little Rock and six more directing a YMCA in Miami, Florida. Late in life, he became a self-taught potter whose pieces were in high demand. Leveritt had two sons and in 2000 was honored by UAM as the recipient of the university's Alumni Award for Achievement and Merit. At the time he was interviewed for this book in the fall of 2010, he was living quietly in Benton, Arkansas, with his long-time companion, Ann Rogers. He died July 12, 2013 at the age of 96.

As for the tales surrounding the Wandering Weevils, Leveritt simply grinned and with a twinkle in his eye, said "I neither deny nor confirm anything."

Buddy Carson was eventually called to active duty by the Army Air Corps and sent to England where he became a B-17 pilot. Carson flew 36 bombing missions over Europe and won the Distinguished Flying Cross before returning to Monticello where he took over his father's grocery store and lived quietly with Elloise, raising two children. Elloise passed away in 2007. "Mr. Buddy," as he was known in Monticello, was a beloved figure in the community and at the university. He never missed a Boll Weevil home game, was a regular at the pre-game tailgate parties and played golf when the weather and his health would permit. He died peacefully on September 28, 2012, at the age of 91.

After leaving A&M, Stewart Ferguson spent two years as a Navy ground school instructor at Louisiana State Normal School in Natchitoches, La., before returning to South Dakota in 1944 to become the head football coach at Deadwood High School. He also coached the basketball and track teams and taught history while enduring a lengthy battle with lung cancer. He died of a heart attack on December 29, 1955. He was 55.

Ferguson's football teams at Deadwood never experienced a losing season and following his death, the playing field at Deadwood High School was renamed Ferguson Memorial Field in his honor, a name it still bears. In 1994, he was enshrined into the South Dakota Sports Hall of Fame.

The architect of college football's strangest team, the man who thumbed his nose at the football establishment, was a bundle of contradictions and insecurities. As a young man, Ferguson bridled at the strict discipline of his minister father and seemed bent on defying authority of any kind. His coaching career is a Jekyll and Hyde tale of a man who, in the beginning, would do anything to win and pad his own ego. In his unpublished memoir, *A Fool Is Born,* (unpublished because Ferguson refused to let editors change a word of his florid text) he takes himself to task for his willingness to break rules and gain any edge in the pursuit of victory on the field.

Away from football, Ferguson was obsessed with the opposite sex. His memoir is full of sexual innuendo and inappropriate references. He described two buildings on the campus of Dakota Wesleyan as "resembling the aroused tits of a middle-aged virgin." He wrote in lurid detail of his experiences working for a middle-aged widow while attending Dakota Wesleyan and described an encounter with a prostitute on the train from South Dakota to Louisiana in similar language.

The question remains – why did Stewart Ferguson do the unthinkable and turn college football from serious sport to comedy? Ferguson was hurt deeply after being fired by Dakota Wesleyan. By the time he was relieved of his coaching duties at Arkansas A&M in 1934, Ferguson was a bitter shell of the ego-driven, referee-baiting firebrand he was at the start of his career. When he resumed coaching at A&M in 1938, he was a changed man.

Turning a football game from serious sport to farce was far beyond Ferguson's original intent when he said – in rule number two of his guidelines for the football program – that the game should be played for the fun in it. When Ferguson created those guidelines, not even he had envisioned turning his football team into a traveling vaudeville show. In his unpublished memoir, Ferguson referred to the idea as coming to him "like steam rising from a manure pile on a cold winter morning."

Ferguson had come to believe that the all-out effort to win when a team was overmatched was futile and psychologically harmful to the players. "To try to win with all-out effort and hopelessly fail is not healthy," Ferguson wrote. "To consistently accomplish things within one's abilities is. The aim is always higher than the battles won. Football should mean more to players, coaches, and even college presidents than a climb toward a championship. If the game cannot be used as an ethical and educational tool for the making of the kind of citizens we want, then it does not belong in the training program for youth that is paid for by the tax payers."

Ferguson, the South Dakota Yankee, went so far as to invoke the most sainted of Southern icons when he wrote "There are still plenty of us left, though, who believe with Robert E. Lee that no war nor anything else is worth either winning or losing except as gentlemen. No victory in even football could be worth more."

Ferguson blamed football for his own character flaws. "I've never had much use for the character I developed while playing football," he wrote. "In fact, that development of my character has likely caused me most of my troubles in living."

Ferguson never considered himself a pioneer or a reformer. "I do not believe that I am a fanatical, glory-hallelujahing reformer in anything," Ferguson wrote. "Even though our football was considered crazy by some people, I doubt if it was any more so than making a game the ultimate thing in the lives of youth and coaching viciously toward the winning of it . . . Many may never know what I am trying to describe. I can't put it in words, but I saw it many times in the faces of my Boll Weevil players. I guess that's the real reason we went crazy in football. Who cares about scores when your eyes are shining."

EPILOGUE

Could it happen today?

Could a team like the Wandering Weevils survive in modern college football's cutthroat environment? Could a coach like Stewart Ferguson thumb his nose at the media, the fans, and the college football establishment and turn the serious business of college football into a whimsical farce?

Not likely.

You'd be hard-pressed to find a coach with Ferguson's mindset, a man willing to turn convention upside down, an original thinker who puts the interest and well-being of his players ahead of victories on the field. Next, you'd need a university president and athletic director secure enough in their posts to allow the coach a free hand in running the football program and who shared their coach's view of athletics and the importance (or lack thereof) of winning.

Would such a team be able to find opponents willing to accept an easy win while being mocked by a bunch of clowns? Would today's game officials play along, or would they strictly enforce the rules?

"I don't guess there's any rule about driving to your opponent's goal line and punting backwards," says David Worlock, director of public relations for the NCAA and associate director of the NCAA

Division I men's basketball tournament. "The game officials might have a problem with riding bicycles onto the field or players removing their helmets during plays. I'm not sure the NCAA would, or could, do much about what happens in a game unless it was a playoff game run directly by the NCAA. The individual conferences would probably sanction a team like that."

Stephen K. Figler, author of *Going the Distance* and *Sport and Play In American Life*, calls Stewart Ferguson "an excellent coach and an outstanding educator. He just didn't do things the conventional way.

"Some of the things that are going on now in big-time college football – buying players, forging transcripts – were going on in the 1930s. In fact, some of it was going on (at UAM). This school was on the verge of dropping intercollegiate football before Ferguson came along and cleaned up the program. That's why I think he was such a unique and interesting character. He was willing to take chances when other people weren't. A lot of us have values, but we're not willing to back them up. Ferguson was."

The story of Stewart Ferguson and the Wandering Weevils serves as a stark reminder of just how much college football has changed since those last carefree days before World War II. Ferguson's boys never received "$100 handshakes" from overzealous boosters, didn't receive new cars paid for by anonymous benefactors, and didn't play the game with one eye on a career in the NFL. Their fathers didn't shop them to the highest bidder, and while they weren't saints, their names didn't end up on a police blotter.

Wise-cracking Tunis Bishop, sleepy-eyed Coy Brown, handsome Carleton Spears and the rest of the Wandering Weevils played the game purely for fun. The few that were left to be interviewed for this book – Buddy Carson, J.P. Leveritt, Eddie MacMillan – remembered their days as gridiron clowns with fondness.

182

"We really didn't care that we were losing," remembered Carson. "Just look at the places we went, the things we saw. I wouldn't have traded that for anything."

The 1939 Wandering Weevils

Player	Position	Class	Hometown
Coy Brown (Captain)	Guard	Senior	Levy, Arkansas
Carleton Spears (Co-Captain)	Halfback	Senior	Clarendon, Arkansas
Boyd Arnold	Halfback	Senior	Bearden, Arkansas
John T. Arnold	Guard	Junior	Pine Bluff, Arkansas
Sam Bateman	Center		
Buell Bishop	Halfback	Freshman	Little, Rock, Arkansas
Tunis Bishop	Halfback	Freshman	Little Rock, Arkansas
Worth Bruner	Center	Sophomore	Mineola, Texas
Pete Cheshier	Halfback	Freshman	Monticello, Arkansas
Stanley Cheshier	End	Sophomore	Monticello, Arkansas
Joe Cook	Guard		
Buddy Crook	Halfback	Freshman	McGehee, Arkansas
Ted Douglass	Halfback		
Terry Field	End	Sophomore	Little Rock, Arkansas
Stan Gilzow	Guard		
T. L. Godfrey	Left End	Sophomore	Dumas, Arkansas
Thomas Hooker	Guard	Sophomore	Pine Bluff, Arkansas
Collier Jordan	Center	Senior	Vernon, Alabama
J. P. Leveritt	End	Junior	Smackover, Arkansas
Robert Maskell	End	Sophomore	Booneville, Arkansas
Eddie McMillan	Guard	Junior	Parkdale, Arkansas
Loy Perry	End	Sophomore	Pine Bluff, Arkansas
James "Annie" Robinson	Quarterback	Freshman	Little Rock, Arkansas
James "Preacher" Sewell	Tackle	Junior	Wilmar, Arkansas
Paul Stegall	Tackle	Sophomore	Monticello, Arkansas
John Strange	Guard	Freshman	El Dorado, Arkansas
George Tillery	End	Sophomore	El Dorado, Arkansas
Winfred Whalen	Halfback	Freshman	Smackover, Arkansas

THE 1940 WANDERING WEEVILS

Player	Position	Class	Hometown
Audis Barringer	Tackle	Freshman	New Edinburg, Arkansas
Tunis Bishop	Halfback	Sophomore	Little Rock, Arkansas
Van Brewer	Center	Senior	Cotton Plant, Mississippi
Worth Bruner	Center	Junior	Mineola, Texas
Frank "Buddy" Carson, Jr.	Halfback	Freshman	Monticello, Arkansas
Pete Cheshier	Quarterback	Sophomore	Monticello, Arkansas
Stanley Cheshier	End	Junior	Monticello, Arkansas
Charles Colvin	Tackle	Freshman	Bernice, Louisiana
J. R. Cubage	Halfback	Freshman	Fordyce, Arkansas
Terry Field	End	Junior	Little Rock, Arkansas
Benny Gaston	Halfback	Freshman	McGehee, Arkansas
Verl Gill	Halfback	Freshman	Monticello, Arkansas
Jewell Grider	Guard		El Dorado, Arkansas
James Hill	Halfback		Parkdale, Arkansas
Ira Jones	Guard		Helena, Arkansas
J. P. Leveritt	End	Senior	Smackover, Arkansas
Robert Maskell	End	Junior	Booneville, Arkansas
Teddy McKinney	Halfback		Rison, Arkansas
John Scritchfield	Guard		El Dorado, Arkansas
Paul Stegall	Tackle	Junior	Monticello, Arkansas
Ralph Stegall	End	Junior	Monticello, Arkansas
George Tolson	Center	Freshman	Rison, Arkansas
Norman Wells	End	Sophomore	Hamburg, Arkansas

Bus Drivers: Alvin Beverburg, Herman Beverburg, Joe Coker

The 1941 Wandering Weevils

Player	Position	Class	Hometown
Williams Bowers	Guard	Freshman	Lamar, Missouri
Frank "Buddy" Carson, Jr.	Halfback	Sophomore	Monticello, Arkansas
Charles Colvin	Tackle	Sophomore	Bernice, Louisiana
Lester "Yank" Corwin	Halfback	Freshman	Long Island, New York
Oscar Dove	Center	Freshman	El Dorado, Arkansas
Benny Gaston	Halfback	Sophomore	McGehee, Arkansas
George "Bud" Heroman	Fullback	Freshman	Monticello, Arkansas
Rex Hoy	Center	Freshman	Smackover, Arkansas
Arthur Isch	Tackle	Sophomore	McGehee, Arkansas
Eugene "Crack" Jackson	End	Sophomore	Bearden, Arkansas
Lawrence "The Stork" Lavender	End		Pine Bluff, Arkansas
Ples "Pete" McDonald	Halfback	Freshman	Gillett, Arkansas
Jimmie "Twig" Moore	End	Freshman	Gould, Arkansas
William "Wild Bill" Owen	Fullback	Freshman	Pine Bluff, Arkansas
Robert Potter	Guard	Freshman	Lamar, Missouri
John "Scritch" Scritchfield	Guard		El Dorado, Arkansas
Paul Stegall (Captain)	Tackle	Junior	Monticello, Arkansas
Bix Stillwell	Halfback	Sophomore	Pine Bluff, Arkansas
Hilburn "Fuzzy" Watts	Guard		Pine Bluff, Arkansas

Bus Drivers: Alvin Beverburg, Herman Beverburg, Joe Coker

BIBLIOGRAPHY

ARTICLES

Clary, Jack. "Winning Isn't Everything . . .," *Touchdown Illustrated,* 1994

Ferguson, Stewart A. "A Fool Is Born," unpublished manuscript

Holley, Donald. "Stewart Ferguson, the Wandering Weevils, and Why They Played Football for Fun," *Drew County Historical Journal,* 1998

Julin, Suzanne. "Edna Ferguson Robinson Interview," *City of Deadwood Oral History Project*, May 16, 2007

BOOKS

The Boll Weevil, 1939

The Boll Weevil, 1940

The Boll Weevil, 1941

Holley, Donald. *Celebrating a Century of Opportunity: From the Fourth District Agricultural School to the University of Arkansas at Monticello.* Reedy Press, 2009

MAGAZINES

Collier's (Nov. 23, 1940): "Football is for Fun," Kyle Crichton

Hofstra Football Magazine, The Official Game Program for Hofstra College home football games (Nov. 16, 1940)

The Humboldt Gridiron (Oct. 23, 1940)

Memphis Flyer (Nov. 11, 1999): "The Marx Brothers of Football," Finger, Michael

Newsweek (Dec. 1, 1941): "The Wandering Weevils"

Nevada Football Magazine (Oct. 19, 1940): "Today's Game, Wolves vs. Boll Weevils"

Sports Illustrated (Sept. 8, 1971): "Winning Wasn't Anything," Frank X. Tolbert

UAM Magazine (Fall 1999): "Mad Genius . . . or 'Damn Fool," Brewer, Jim

NEWSPAPERS

Ann Arbor News (Oct. 1, 1941): "Boll Weevils of Arkansas A. & M. Hold Workout At Ferry Field; Use Swing-Gate Offense," Marsh, Mill

Ann Arbor News (Oct. 1, 1941): "Boll Weevils Practice Their Handsprings"

Arkansas Democrat (Nov. 17, 1939): "Weevils Win on Homecoming"

Arkansas Democrat (May 10, 1940): "Boll Weevils To See The Country"

Arkansas Democrat (September 15, 1940): "Football for Fun Becoming Profitable, Traveling Boll Weevils Expect to Make More Than $10,000 This Year," Jack Keady

Arkansas Gazette (Sept. 30, 1939): "Boll Weevils Defeated At Philadelphia"

Arkansas Gazette (Nov. 4, 1939): "Boll Weevils Lose to Rolla Miners, 28-13"

Arkansas Gazette (Nov. 12, 1939): "Weevils Take 49-7 Licking At Cleveland"

Arkansas Gazette (Nov. 17, 1939): "A. & M. Wins Homecoming Game, 26-6"

Arkansas Gazette (Sept. 8, 1940): "Gazette Sports Gazing," Ben Epstein

Arkansas Gazette (Sept. 9, 1940): "40 Candidates For Weevil Eleven"

Arkansas Gazette (Oct. 6, 1940): "Bollweevils Lose, 28-6, To Lebanon"

Arkansas Gazette (Nov. 1, 1940): "Aggies Take On Hendrix Today In First Home Stand"

Arkansas Gazette (Nov. 2, 1940): "Bollweevils Hold Hendrix To 7-0 Score"

Arkansas Gazette (July 3, 1980): "1939-41 'Wandering Weevils' Dazzled Crowds From Coast to Coast," Brewer, Jim

Asheville Citizen (Setp. 28, 1941): "Arkansas Aggies 'Clown' Against Lions Here Tonight"

Atlanta Constitution (Oct. 13, 1941): "Wandering Arkansas Weevils Play Only When Mood Strikes"

Atlanta Journal (Oct. 26, 1941): "Zany Weevils To Travel 8,000 Miles"

Belleville (Wis.) Recorder (Oct. 16, 1941): "Strange As It Seems," John Hix

Bethlehem Evening Bulletin (Oct. 31, 1941): "Close-ups On Sports," Lynn C. Doyle

Bethlehem Globe-Times (Oct. 31, 1941): "Moravians Roll To Easy Victory"

The Birmingham Post (March 30, 1940): "Something New—Something Different, This Grid Game"

The Charleston Daily Mail (Oct. 4, 1939): "Tricky Passing Attack Puzzles Rival Teams"

The Charleston Daily Mail (Oct. 6, 1939): "Morris Harvey Ready For Passing Attack, Ward Afraid Razzle-Dazzle Offense Of Invaders Will Baffle Locals"

The Charleston Daily Mail (Oct. 7, 1939): "Eagles Trample A. and M. 33-0"

The Charleston Gazette (Oct. 6, 1939): "Eagles Face Dazzling Air Attack in A. and M. Game"

Christian Science Monitor (Oct. 27, 1941): "Football's Vagabonds"

The Cincinnati Enquirer (Nov. 12, 1939): "Carroll Wins 49-7; Wild Show Put On By Arkansas A&M"

The Cleveland News (Nov. 8, 1939): "All Up for A&M," Sport Trail by James E. Doyle

The Cleveland Plain Dealer (Nov. 7, 1939): "Arkansas A&M Gives Football Back to Boys: Haven't Won in 2 Year — and Don't Care," Gordon Cobbledick

The Cleveland Plain Dealer (Nov. 9, 1939): "Carroll and Cats Both Point For Big Four Grid Battle"

The Cleveland News (Nov. 10, 1939): "Stadium to Be Site of Unusual Grid Game Tomorrow," Isi Newborn

The Cleveland Press (Nov. 10, 1939): "Arkansas' Famous Boll Weevils Arrive for Game, Arkansawyer Strategy Includes Their 'Swinging Gate' Formation," Frank Gibbons

The Cleveland News (Nov. 10, 1939): "Arkansas Aggies Throw All the Passes But Opponents, Alas, Win All the Games," Ed McAuley

The Cleveland Plain Dealer (Nov. 11, 1939): "These Arkansas Travelers Play Football for Fun"

The Cleveland News (Nov. 12, 1939): "Carroll Deals 49-7 Drubbing To Arkansans"

The Cleveland Plain Dealer (Nov. 12, 1939): "Carroll Crushes Arkansas A&M Eleven, 49 to 7"

The Cleveland Plain Dealer (Nov. 12, 1939): "Blue Streaks Rip Arkansas A&M For Two Periods," Gordon Cobbledick

The Columbus Dispatch (Nov. 12, 1939): "Aggies Score On Carroll"

Danville (Va.) Register (Oct. 25, 1941): "Arkansas Aggies Leave On 32 Day Trip That Will Take Them Over 8,000 Miles"

Dayton Daily News (Sept. 30, 1941): "Arkansas Travelers In Person Here"

Denton Texas Record-Chronicle (Oct. 8, 1940): Eagles Face Arkansas Grid Travellers (sic) Here This Week"

Denton (Tex.) Record-Chronicle (Oct. 11, 1941): "Eagles Again Overrun Arkansas Boll Weevils To Take Victory 60 to 0"

Dumas (Ark.) Clarion (Nov. 18, 1970): "Stu Ferguson's Football Was Fun," Schexnayder, Charlotte

Eau Claire (Wis.) Leader (Oct. 26, 1941): "Grid Vagabonds Leave on 32-Day Football Journey"

Elkins (W. Va.) Inter-Mountain (Nov. 13, 1941): "Colorful Arkansas A. M. Team Plays Here Saturday"

The Evansville Courier (Nov. 18, 1941): "Marx Bros. of Football Vs. Evansville College Saturday, Football's Fun-Makers Are In City"

The Evansville Courier (Nov. 22, 1941): "Here's a Football Coach Minus Gray Hair From Worry," Dick Anderson

The Evansville Sunday Courier and Press (Nov. 23, 1941): "Evansville Rips Boll Weevils 26-6, In Grid 'Hellzapoppin'"

Fort Worth Star Telegraph (Oct. 11, 1941): "Ah, Fergie May Realize His Dream," Francis X. Tolbert

Forth Worth Star Telegraph (Oct. 12, 1941) "Worst of All the Boll Weevils Holds North Texas to 60-0!" Francis X. Tolbert

The Harrisburg (Pa.) Evening News (Oct. 1, 1940): "Farcical Football For Fun-Loving Fans . . . Foils Financial Fiasco," Eddie Beachler

The Harrisburg (Pa.) Evening News (Oct. 3, 1940): "Arkansas Eleven Reaches Scene"

The Harrisburg (Pa.) Patriot (Oct. 3, 1940): "College Game At Hershey"

Humboldt Standard (Oct. 19, 1940): "Arkansas and Humboldt Staters Meet Wednesday Night"

The Johnstown Tribune (Nov. 7, 1941): "Football's Craziest Team To Tangle With St. Francis"

Lebanon Valley (Pa.) Post (Oct. 3, 1940): "Arkansas A&M Seeks Its Second Victory In Three Years"

Lebanon Valley (Pa.) Post (Oct. 4, 1940): "In Reverse," Jack Conlin

Los Angeles Times (October 17, 1940): "Sport Postscripts," Paul Zimmerman

Louisville Courier Journal (Sept. 28, 1940): "Arkansas A&M Practices Here"

Memphis Press Scimitar (Oct. 14, 1941): "Those Arkansas Boll Weevils Again," Eldon Roark

The Mitchell Daily Republic (Sept. 24, 1940): "Hardrockers Are Braced For Tilt With 'Fun Team'"

The Mobile Register (Oct. 8, 1941): "Spring Hill Badgers Play National Prankster Team, Arkansas A. & M., Tonight"

The Mobile Register (Oct. 8, 1941): "Good Morning," Vincent Johnson

The Monticellonian (Nov. 2, 1940): "Local Weevil Players Like To Play For Fun"

Nassau Review-Star (Nov. 15, 1940): "Dutchmen Make Last Home Stand Of Year Against Colorful Boll Weevils"

Nevada State Journal (Oct. 14, 1940): "Arkansas Boll Weevils Are Most Unorthodox Grid Team"

Nevada State Journal (Oct. 15, 1940): "Football for Fun Brings Headlines to Boll Weevils"

Nevada State Journal (Oct. 16, 1940): "Daffy Arkansas Aggies' Gridiron Crew Billed As 'Marx Brothers Of Football. Boll Weevils' Flaunt Tradition Of Gridiron Lore"

Nevada State Journal (Oct. 17, 1940): "Screwball Arkansas Aggies Located! They're in L. A., Due Here Tomorrow"

Nevada State Journal (Oct. 18, 1940): "Clowning Visitors Are Underdogs in Homecoming Event"

Newark Evening News (Oct. 31, 1941): "Victoryless Boll Weevils Get 'Lot of Fun' Out Of Losing"

Newark Evening News (Nov. 1, 1941): "Sports in The News," Jimmie Eben

Newark Star-Ledger (Nov. 1, 1941): "Upsala Gets First Win Over 'Daffiness Boys'"

Newark Star-Ledger (Nov. 1, 1941): "Upsala Pilot Exhorts Weevils to 'Shoot Works' Against Own Team"

Newark Sunday Call (Nov. 2, 1941): "Upsala College Cracks 'Nuttiest' Team to Score First Win, 19 to 6"

New York Post (Oct. 30, 1941): "College Grapevine," Herbert Allen

New York Post (Nov. 13, 1941)

The Odessa News-Times (Oct. 12, 1939): "Daniel Baker Will Be Playing Against Some Colorful Gridders

From Arkansas, 38 Year Old Preacher Plays Tackle," Bob Nash

The Odessa News-Times (Oct. 13, 1939): "Unorthodox Style Of Play Used By Men From Monticello May Upset Hill Billies From Baker"

The Odessa News-Times (Oct. 14, 1939): "Daniel Baker Wins, 33-13 From Weevils"

Peoria Journal-Transcript (Oct. 2, 1941): "Weevils Devise New Nonsense"

Peoria Journal-Transcript (Oct. 2, 1941): "Marx Brothers Of Football To Play Tech At Stadium Tonight," Perry, Russell

Philadelphia Inquirer (Sept. 29, 1940): "Hawk eleven Starts Home Card Today"

Philadelphia Inquirer (Sept. 29, 1940): "All For Fun Team From Arkansas Is Hawks' Opponent, Sightseeing Gridders Don't Give a Hoot Who Wins Today's Tussle," Hugh Kolbmann

Philadelphia Record (Sept. 29, 1939): "St. Joseph's Meets Strong Aggies Team"

The Pottsville (Pa.) Evening Republic (Nov. 7, 1941): "Wandering Boll Weevils Wander Into Pottsville"

The Rapid City Daily Journal (Oct. 29, 1940): "Gridders Trim Hardrockers, 26-7"

Reno Evening Gazette (Oct. 18, 1940): "WOlfpack to Battle Arkansas Aggie Team In Homecoming Game, Nevada Favored Over Invading Boll Weevil Eleven"

The Richmond (Ky.) Daily Register (Sept. 28, 1940): "Maroon Foe Saturday In Unique Team"

Richmond (Va.) Times-Dispatch (Oct. 25, 1941): "Wandering Arkansas Weevils Set Out on Record Grid Trip"

The Rolla News (Nov. 4, 1939): "Miners And Arkansas To Play Today"

St. Louis Post Dispatch (Nov. 11, 1941): "Not All Nuts the Kind You Crack With Your Teeth, Football Shows"

The Sioux Falls Daily Argus Leader (Sept. 24, 1940): "Former Dakotan, Most Envied Coach in United States, Brings Screwiest Grid Eleven Back for Homecoming This Week"

The Sioux Falls Daily Argus Leader (Sept. 25, 1940): "Little Fergy (Remember Him?) Preaches Fun Football, Just Tells Boys Rules, Turns 'Em Loose in Ten States"

Springfield Daily News (Nov. 17, 1940): "Barnstorming Arkansas 'Boll Weevils' Caper Against Champion Bears Thursday Morning"

Tulsa Daily World (March 30, 1940): "Arkansas Aggie Grid Coach Doesn't Have to Win to Hold His Job"

Utica (N.Y.) Press (Oct. 25, 1941): "Weevils Off on 8,000 Mile Tour Wearing Sample Grid Jerseys"

Weevil Outlet (Undated): "A. and M. to See the United States by Football

Weevil Outlet (April 30, 1939): "Ferguson Completes Ambitious Intersectional Schedule"

Weevil Outlet (Undated): "Wandering Weevils To Get Nationwide Publicity"

PERSONAL INTERVIEWS

Carson, Frank Jr., Joseph P. Leveritt, Thomas Edward "Eddie Mac" MacMillan

CPSIA information can be obtained
at www.ICGtesting.com
Printed in the USA
LVHW090526280821
696315LV00002B/81